# THE QUOTABLE TRUMAN

# THE QUOTABLE TRUMAN

Edited by David Gallen

Carroll & Graf Publishers, Inc.
New York

Compilation copyright © 1994 by David Gallen

First Carroll & Graf edition 1994

Carroll & Graf Publishers, Inc.
260 Fifth Avenue
New York, NY 10001

Library of Congress Cataloging-in-Publication Data
Truman, Harry S., 1884–1972.
    The quotable Truman / compiled by David Gallen.—
  1st Carroll & Graf ed.
        p.      cm.
    ISBN 0-7867-0133-1 : $19.95
    1. United States—Politics and government—
  Quotations, maxims. etc. 2. Truman, Harry S.,
  1884–1972—Quotations. I. Gallen, David. II. Title.
E742.5.T62   1994
973.918'092—dc20                              94-26428
                                                  CIP

Manufactured in the United States of America

Courtesy Harry S. Truman Library

*With special thanks
to Elizabeth Safly and the staff
of the Harry S. Truman Library
in Independence, Missouri*

# Contents

# Contents

# Preface

In a series of interviews recorded over a six-month period, from the end of June 1960 to January 31, 1961, retired President Harry S. Truman discussed the history of the United States government, its Constitution, and the presidency at his home in Missouri. During the same period the Democratic candidate for president, John Kennedy, defeated Richard Nixon, then vice president to Dwight D. Eisenhower, in the national election of 1960. The election results, which ended the eight-year tenure of Republicans in the White House, cannot have disappointed Truman, who once said of his successor that Eisenhower didn't know anything when he came to office and didn't learn anything while he was there.

Truman places Eisenhower among the "do-nothing, sit-still presidents" as opposed to those men who fully exercised the powers granted them by the Constitution because they "understood the presidency for what it is: the chief executive of the

xi

greatest republic in the history of the world."
Throughout the interviews Truman has much to
say about the responsibilities of the chief executive
in our republic, and what he has to say he says
frankly, sometimes bluntly, as he shows how some
of the men who have held the most powerful office
in the nation have decisively run it while others
decidedly have fumbled it.

Truman was planning eventually to write a history of the United States presidency based on the
1960 interviews. He wanted to write a book, he
said, that would arouse the curiosity of young people in particular, one that would spur them on to
study further the men and events that had shaped
their nation. ("Men make history, history doesn't
make men," says Truman without question, quali-
fication, doubt, or political correctness.) He intended, too, that the book give "some idea of what
went on in the formative stages of our republic,
which finally turned out to be the greatest free
country in the history of the world" and that it
provide a history of the Constitution and the government "in a way that the ordinary fellow can
easily understand." The taped interviews, then,
were merely groundwork, but the history itself was
never written.

The transcripts of the recordings for a "Proposed
History of the American Presidency, 1787–1945"
contain more than plans and intentions, however.
They offer Truman's perspective on the early history of the American republic as he explores the
pursuit of liberty, defines the tradition of free government, and illuminates the objectives of the Constitution. They record many anecdotes, much
opinion, terse analysis, and a lot of common sense.

They take Truman through the roll of thirty-four presidents. They catch him in expansive moods as well as in moments of reflection, and if the temper is occasionally short, it is never ill. They display ample humor and homespun wit. And they demonstrate again and again that our thirty-third president is certainly quotable.

*The Quotable Truman* comprises excerpts from the interview transcripts that have been arranged and edited to introduce the reader to Truman's views on the major topics he proposed for his history: the founding of the republic, the Constitution, the presidents and the presidency, the nation's westward expansion. It includes Truman's comment on other, related matters, because along the way you can't overlook, he says, "some of the things that were done that were not morally correct, particularly with regard to the Indian inhabitants of this country. And in the wasting of natural resources on the part of these people who are always trying to exploit the welfare of the country for their own personal benefit."

Several times in the transcripts Truman refers to the men who became millionaires by ruthlessly exploiting the land and the people. He remarks, for instance, "the way old Andrew Carnegie got rich . . . by pounding down the people who made steel for him. And then, of course, when he died, he died so rich I think his conscience hurt him and he left a lot of money for libraries." The exploitation of the many for the wealth of a few does not sit well with Harry Truman. Indeed, throughout the transcripts he voices his distrust of a financial aristocracy, of special privilege, of economic royalists. You can always expect resistance from "the old conservative

outfits ... when there's a change for the welfare
and benefit of the ordinary fellow," he says. Probably the most recurrent phrase throughout the interviews is "the welfare and benefit of the people."
It clearly defines Truman's political position as a
man for the people.

Not that the people are without their faults.
"There are too many lazy people in the country,"
Truman asserts, too many who let others act in
their interests and do their thinking for them. He
notes, too, that "the people always get tired when
a strong president is in office and tells them what
they ought to do for their own good, and makes
them do it. They don't like it. They like to quit."
They also usually vote for the other party at the
end of a strong administration, he observes.

As president, Truman not only spoke for the people; he also spoke as a man of the people. When he
describes Lincoln as "just a good ordinary citizen of
the United States" or sees him as "one of the people—and he wanted to stay that way," he could
very well be talking about himself. Lincoln, he
says, is the sort of man you can admire because he
was "just himself." Then he adds, "There is nothing
in the world I dislike more than a stuffed shirt."
Truman had little time for pretension. He spoke
plainly, and was known as the president with the
"common touch."

Common or not, he was also the president who
ended the war with Japan, rehabilitated postwar
Europe with the Marshall Plan, authorized the
Berlin Airlift, faced down the USSR in Greece and
Turkey, fought the Korean War, and then chose
not to run for reelection in 1952. Throughout his
administration he made difficult decisions; good

presidents have to, as he shows us in many of the excerpts in this book. In others he foresees major problems in Southeast Asia and predicts a crisis in American cities. For the most part, though, he speaks not as a prophet but as a witness to history and as an historian. He recalls learning of the un-expected Democratic nomination of Woodrow Wil-son in 1912 by telegraph, and he remembers what he was doing the day that President McKinley was shot in Buffalo. ("I have always said that if I ever caught a fellow that was trying to shoot me, I would stick the gun down his throat and pull the trigger," snaps Truman elsewhere in the tran-scripts.) He also talks about dirty politics, Ameri-can heroes, smart-aleck liberals, the Civil War, trusting the Russians, witch hunts, Geronimo, in-come tax, and doctors. And he talks about the wel-fare and benefit of the people.

The voice is not hollow, the shirt is not stuffed.

# PART I

## Some Thoughts on Freedom, Dissent, Democracy, and the Founding of the Republic

## The Worst Thing in the World:
## A Prefatory Note

One of the things you've got to give the Greeks
and early Romans credit for: They gave everyone
a chance to think as he thought was right and they
didn't persecute him, or hang him, or burn him, or
anything of the kind. That only happened when the
Christians were in control—so-called Christians.

All this trouble, brainwashing and things of that
kind, started with Loyola and the establishment of
the Spanish Inquisition, and if you remember, they
put Galileo in jail because he said the world was
round, which was against the religious teachings
at that time. And you'll find that most all of the
tortures in Communist countries and others where
people believe in the control of thought originated
under the program that was set up by Loyola and
the Spanish Inquisition, which was one of the most
terrible things that ever happened to the world.

**Persecution for freedom of thought is the
worst thing that ever happened in the history
of the world.**

3

*The discovery of America was not really a happenstance, if you look at the history of navigation over a long period. It was brought about by the persistence of one man who believed that the world was round and who wanted to prove it. His name was Christopher Columbus and he never got the credit entitled to him.*

*The only thing that was new about the new world was that it was a place to go to get away from oppression.*

## SEEKING LIBERTY

The settlement of the eastern coast of what later became the United States was brought about to some extent by an idea on the part of the four great European powers—Spain, France, Holland, and Britain—to have a hand in the opening up of the

Western Hemisphere and to some extent by oppression and especially religious persecution.

And that's the reason they came over here—the Dutch, the French, the Spaniards, the Swedes, the British. All the people who came to the east coast of the United States, except the Spaniards, were escaping oppression. They were thinking about what really constituted human liberty. But after they got here, they turned out in some instances to be just as oppressive as the people they had left.

## Colonizing America: Dissenters and Dissent

A funny thing about the whole business is that when these English dissenters came over here they were just as strong against other dissenters as the Church of England or Cromwell had been against them.

In Virginia the old established Anglican church was set up because they were the people that were chased out of England when Charles I got his head cut off [in 1649] and Cromwell and the Puritans took over.

And when the Roman Catholics came over with Lord Baltimore [in 1632] and established Roman Catholic settlements in Maryland, they also established freedom of worship, to protect themselves, because there were so many Protestants in the colonies.

The New Englanders were all dissenters. They didn't believe in the established church. They didn't want to conform to the Church of England as it was set up under Queen Elizabeth or James I, who succeeded her. And the people who were in

6

charge seemed to hold the opinion that they were closer to the Almighty than anybody else—which isn't true at all; I don't think that any man has got a closer approach to the Almighty than the ordinary individual—and that they could enforce law in New England as they saw it, according to their religion. That's the reason Roger Williams had to flee Massachusetts and went down to Rhode Island and established freedom of worship there.

It's most interesting that the dissenters—the Methodists and Baptists and Presbyterians—finally set up their own arrangement and were just as mean to the people who didn't believe with them as the others were. So what are you going to do?

### Getting Together: The Freedom to Dissent

The Puritans in New England, and in New Jersey the Swedes, in New York the Dutch, and in Maryland the Catholics from England under Lord Baltimore, and in Virginia those who had been overcome by Cromwell, and the French in South Carolina—most of them had been persecuted at home and that is the reason they came out with a government based on freedom of religion, freedom of politics, and freedom of action for the individual.

But it took them from 1608 and 1620 up until 1760 before they began to get together. That is a long time. That was on account of transportation and communication. Back then it took five or six days to go from Baltimore to New York. Now you can do it in half an hour.

*David Gallen*

## *Meeting Halfway: The Melting Pot*

The fact is that when these people had to associate with one another—when the Quakers in Pennsylvania had to associate with the Catholics in Maryland and when the high-hats down in Virginia had to associate with the lowbrows in Massachusetts—they became acquainted with each other and found out that there wasn't any real difference between them, or that what they had in common was stronger. That's how the melting pot was brought about.

And later when the settlement of the West took place it was made up of a cross section from all those peoples, and they never had any idea of cutting anybody's throat because his religious beliefs were a little different from what they themselves believed.

## *Tolerating Difference: An Observation*

The theologists, you know, are like all the rest of the crackpot high-hats. They have a certain approach to things, but all you have to do is to read the Sermon on the Mount and to read the Ten Commandments and the laws in Leviticus and to read Deuteronomy and you'll find out: **It's the heart of the man himself that makes things great.**

The Sermon on the Mount is the greatest document for a lesson on how to get along that I know of, and it's tolerance that counts. A man's ideas of what is right and what is wrong are attained through life and demonstrated in his actions and associations with his neighbors. If he's not a good citizen, they soon find it out and put him where he belongs. If he is, he doesn't have any trouble, and all this theological contest about what this and that means and whether twenty-five hundred angels can stand on the point of a needle is not worth a hoot so far as the welfare of the world is concerned.

********

*"Proclaim Liberty throughout all the Land unto all the Inhabitants Thereof." —Leviticus 25:10*

*If you'll read the inscription on the Liberty Bell [Leviticus 25:10], you'll find out where the first idea of liberty to all the world came about; it came about in the time of Hammurabi and the Egyptian empires. People then were beginning to awake to the fact that they had some reason to want to know how the government was run by the dictators. The same thing will take place in Russia and China.*

## PROCLAIMING LIBERTY

***"Taxation without representation is tyranny."***

I don't think the people who made up the thirteen colonies really wanted to tear themselves loose from the mother country. But the fact that they did tear themselves loose from the mother country

9

did that country more good than any other one thing in the history of the world.

The difficulty was brought about by the French and Indian War. The British government tried to make the colonies pay for the French and Indian War, and they wouldn't do it because they didn't have any representation or say on the tax proposition. That's what caused the whole trouble, taxation without representation. What they really wanted, in the beginning, was representation in the British parliament.

I think the colonists were as loyal as they could be to the British monarchy, but they felt like their rights were being taken away from them by the British government. They had come over here hoping that they could improve their condition both physically and financially, and when the British government continued to exploit the colonies, then they got together to set up their own government through the Continental Congress, which began to meet in 1774, I think.

**I think the best asset the British ever had was the rebellion of the thirteen colonies. It changed the attitude of the British toward the people who are dependent on them.**

### *A Matter of Principle*

Our revolution was fought for representation in government, so that the people could not be taxed except by their own consent. Our revolution was based on the principle that **government is by the consent of the governed.** Had the British king been smart enough to understand that, as two or three of his ministers were, there would never have been any separation between the colonies and the British government.

And before King George knew it he had a situation where a whole band of young men were meeting in Philadelphia, with George Washington presiding and with Benjamin Franklin in an advisory capacity, and working out a document of government which has never been equaled in the history of the world, and that's the Constitution of the United States.

The democratic principles defined in the Constitution had engaged the minds of men before, in the Dutch Republic. It had engaged the minds of men in the original Roman Republic, but they became fat and sassy and wound up with a Roman Empire. And if you study the Greek city-states and study Herod the Great's government in Israel and study what happened in Egypt and those great countries that were the sources of our civilization, you'll find that it took two thousand years until the men at the Constitutional Congress could find out what really amounted to a free government, and we finally got it, and we're lucky indeed to have it.

The young men who wrote this Constitution knew their history. There are very few people nowadays who know as much as they did about former forms of government, that's the trouble.

### A Brief Survey of Democratic Government

In the time of the Judges in Israel there was an idea of justice for the welfare and benefit of the individual.

11

In the Greek city-states that was also true, except that the Greek city-states believed there were two classes of people—those who didn't have to work and those who did. They had slaves. They also had people who had an ideal as to how government ought to be set up. Plato and Socrates always worked with the idea that the individual had his rights, but they believed that there was a certain set of individuals who didn't have any rights.

The Romans had the same idea exactly, they got their ideas from the Greek city-states. The greatest honor that could come to a Roman was to be a citizen—that is, a citizen of the city of Rome—but no matter whether he was a slave or what he was, he had his right under the law to make his appearance and get justice.

But really the fundamental basis for a just government, in my opinion, originated in the Mesopotamian Valley twenty-five hundred years ago or maybe three thousand, five hundred years ago, long before the Greek and the Roman empires came into existence, as you will find if you will read the laws of Hammurabi. The codification of Hammurabi granted individuals the rights of property and the rights to his own life, although they did believe in slavery. It wasn't a classless society; they had nobles and people who were in charge of the government, and in all these countries—Egypt and Mesopotamia and all the rest of them—they had a priesthood who really ran things. They usually came to a violent end, as all those priesthood governments did.

That is why the separation of church and state is fundamental to our Constitution, and it is right,

because in all of history the governments controlled by a religious hierarchy always came to a
bad end.

\*\*\*\*\*\*\*

## PRESERVING LIBERTY

It requires constant watchfulness to preserve liberty, and the Constitution is set up for the purpose
of preserving the liberty of the individual, and
when we cease to understand that that is the case
and let things run and take care of themselves,
then we are in trouble.

### Defining Democracy

You take the word *democracy*. The Russians have
absolutely debauched it. It doesn't mean at all
what the word is set out to mean. It means freedom
of action in government, but the Russians don't
have freedom of action in government, yet they call
themselves a democracy.

**Democracy is a town meeting.** New England
had their town meetings and they had to sit and
argue sometimes to pass one little ordinance to appropriate a nickel. The objective of our setup in
government is in the form of a republic and the
people have just as close an approach to the members of the government who make up that republic
as they have in the so-called democracies. A democ-

racy won't work for the simple reason that a democracy is a nice little town meeting.

**We don't have a democracy. We have checks and balances.** *Republic* applies perfectly to our form of government—a government by representation under a constitution which limits the powers of the three branches of the government to what they are intended to be—judicial, executive, and legislative.

Because our government is a representative republic is the reason that we are the oldest government in the world today, and we'll continue to be as long as we understand that a republic is what we are and not a democracy.

**If it weren't for the fact that democracy was the basis for the whole thing, we wouldn't have a free government, but we have a free government for the simple reason that we have a representative republic.**

**Democracy is nothing but mob rule; a representative government is not mob rule.**

### *Democracy and Demagoguery in the Greek City-States*

There has not been a democracy since the Greek city-states. The Greek city-states could never agree among themselves. They always had to stand up and argue themselves out of the point of operation.

Alcibiades was one of the greatest demagogues that ever hit the Greek states, and he upset the free government of Athens until it finally wound up that Alexander the Great could come along and do what he did. It ended up in a dictatorship.

## Demagogues . . .

Demagogues are rabble-rousers. They know how to appeal to the passions of the people. Huey Long was a demagogue. He tried his best to overturn the government of the United States and set it up just like he had in Louisiana, but it didn't work.

Any demagogue can stir up enough people to cause trouble by taking a side issue and blowing it up. That's what happened with Senator Joe McCarthy. McCarthy was one of the worst demagogues that we ever had in this country—the only man in the history of the country who succeeded in getting himself censored as a United States senator.

## And Demagoguery in the United States

We've gone through periods of hysteria. In Massachusetts religion was used to convict old ladies of being witches, and by the time the legislature passed a bill exonerating them, it was a little too late because most of them had been drowned or shot or hanged or something of that kind.

A hundred years after that in Baltimore a demagogue ran for president on the Anti-Masonic ticket and the Anti-Masons began to tear down Catholic churches and to tar and feather Catholic priests.

Then along came the Ku Klux Klan as a result

15

of the Civil War. It was organized for the purpose of keeping the Negroes from taking charge of the government in the South, and it was revived again in 1920 and it was anti-Catholic, anti-Negro, and anti-Jew. We had a terrible time with it.

The government must be the balance between too much on one side and too much on the other. Whether it is labor unions or whether it is the financial control of all the maneuvers of the government or whether it is some demagogic approach to fool the general public, the government ought to be there to see that there is a proper balance made and the situation is not developed to the point where one organization or one outfit can have complete control of the people of the United States. And I don't think that will ever come about in this country. There are too many of us.

### A Final Note on Demagogues

A demagogue has his uses as well as the rest of the inhabitants of the country. I have been associated with some of the great demagogues of this period. Demagogues start out with a great plan, something that looks like it will be very helpful to the general people, but if they are too demagogic, they will run the thing into the ground, and if they have anything good left over, it will be made to work. Otherwise they are just a passing phenomenon that takes place in any republic.

# PART II

## The Constitution
## & Why It's the Greatest Government
## Document in the History of the World

*"We, the People of the United States, in order to form a more perfect union, establish justice, insure domestic tranquility, provide for the common defence, promote the general welfare, and secure the blessings of liberty to ourselves and our posterity, do ordain and establish this Constitution for the United States of America." —The Preamble*

*The people are the sovereigns of the whole government of the United States. But the sovereignty of the government of the United States is in the president and the legislative branch of the government, the Congress.*

# EXPLORING THE CONSTITUTION

## *The Preamble:*
## *The Difference Between Being Ruled*
## *and Being Governed*

You will find that in their American colonies France and Spain appointed colonial governors with absolute power under the crown, and the people were not represented at all in that government. But the British colonies had royal governors appointed by the British crown and they had legislatures which acted on tax matters and things of that sort. Through all the hundred or hundred and fifty years while these legislatures were operating, the colonials became very well experienced in how to operate a local government and to see that it operated for the welfare and benefit of the people. Everywhere in the local government there was representation of the people and participation by the people.

And that's what finally wound up in the national government of the United States, where complete control of the government resides solely in the people. The Preamble of the Constitution definitely sets that out. It says those powers not delegated in the Constitution remain in the people. It is the difference between being ruled and governed.

**The government, according to the Preamble of the Constitution, is of and by and for the people, and that's all there is to it.**

## The Articles:
## Separating the Powers

The Constitution of the United States is an outline of government which protects the people. It is written in simple language. It states exactly what is meant. The Constitution isn't tangled up with any legal verbiage or any Latin inserts, and when you read it you can read it so you can understand it.

The first article of the Constitution set up the legislative branch of the government and put the purse strings into the hands of the elected branch of the government—that's the House of Representatives. The second article of the document set up an executive with certain powers and duties to enforce the law. The third article of the Constitution gave the United States the authority to set up courts that would pass on the legality of laws that were passed by Congress.

The most powerful man in the government is the president, and the second most powerful is the speaker of the House of Representatives, because he controls the finances, and the chief justice is the third.


## Accomplishing an Objective

In England the English colonists had been living under an absolute monarch, King George III, and the French also, after Napoleon, lived under an absolute monarch, and the people who made up these colonies didn't want to live under an absolute monarch. The makers of the Constitution thought that by the division of the legislative, the executive, and the judicial powers of the country they'd be much less likely to have a dictator. **And that's what the objective of the Constitution is: to prevent a dictatorship.**

### An Observation on Efficiency in Government

**I always say that when there's too much efficiency in government you've got a dictator. And it isn't efficiency in government we're after, it's freedom in government.**

I don't think too much efficiency in government is a good thing, although that doesn't mean that the executive branch of the government ought not to handle things as efficiently as possible. But the legislative and the judicial branch are entirely independent of him, and if the time ever comes when we concentrate all the power for legislating and for justice in one place, then we've got a dictatorship and we go down the drain the same as all the rest of these republics have.

### Balancing the Power

If you have a very strong executive and have leadership in the legislature that can understand what's in view, you won't have any trouble keeping things going for the simple reason that the leadership in both places can get together and work out a program that will work. When you have a weak executive, you can't do that. When you have no leadership in Congress, you can't do that. And of course when the judges decide to pass on things, they sometimes make terrible mistakes, but they can be corrected at a later date.

We've only had one or two chief justices who have passed on things that were purely political. Well, no judge should do that. John Marshall was a political judge. If you'll remember, in one instance old Jackson told the Supreme Court—that is, Marshall—that the chief justice had made his decision, so now let the chief justice enforce it. Had Marshall been a diplomat, he would have approached Jackson to be sure that his decision would be enforced by the president.

*The Constitution has a wonderful preamble— and it's got the word* welfare *in it, and there's another place where the word* welfare *comes up, and it took the Supreme Court one hundred and fifty years to find those two words.*

### The Bill of Rights: Protecting the People

The objective of the Federalists was to set up a strong government, and the objective of those who insisted on the Bill of Rights was to see that that strong government did not in any way impose on the individual.

It was after the articles of the Constitution defining the powers of the government had been set up that it occurred to somebody—and I think Jefferson was the prime mover here—that the protection of the individual from his government had been overlooked. And an individual had to be pro-

tected from his government or we'd just have the
same old go-around that they had in the monarch-
ies in Europe. The first ten amendments to the
Constitution are strictly for the protection of the
individual against the encroachment of the government on his rights—and I don't see where you're
going to draw the line between individual rights
and human rights, there aren't any lines in my
book.

**The primary function of government is to
serve the people.** And to serve them in every
way—economically and socially and every other
way—so that a man can do the things that he
would like to do without interference, and that's
what the first ten amendments guarantee. They
guarantee the individual freedom of thought, freedom of religion, and protection against undue
search and seizure, and the quartering of troops
on anyone's premises without his permission,
which had been happening throughout the colonies
under George III.

The first ten amendments were adopted in 1792
three years after the Constitution was in effect.
They are the greatest part of the Constitution, in
my opinion.

### Amending the Constitution

The Constitution of the United States is not a legislative document. It is an enabling document. The
Constitution provides for legislation by the body
that's authorized and is capable of legislating, and
that's the way it ought to be. And when they make

a legislative document out of the Constitution, it no longer will work.

The great thing about the Constitution is that it provides for its own amendment. When it comes to a point where it won't work under certain conditions, then we have the right to amend it. Although there have been three or four thousand amendments proposed to the Constitution of the United States that would make it a legislative document and absolutely ruin its purpose, they have only passed twenty-two. And they only passed two bad ones in passing those twenty-two (the prohibition amendment and the amendment limiting the president to two terms).

### The Civil Rights Amendments: Unfinished Business

What was decided by the thirteenth, fourteenth, and fifteenth amendments hasn't been settled yet, and it's one of the blots on our international setup, because I'd say that sixty-five or seventy percent of the people in the world are colored—either yellow, black, or red. And there are only between about seven hundred fifty and eight hundred million white people in the world, and the other people have a perfect right to better conditions in the world for their welfare and benefit.

We have got to stop this colored business if we expect to be the leaders of the free world.

*David Gallen*

## Desegregating the Armed Forces: A Start

I made the order to stop segregation in the military services and in other places with the intention of implementing the thirteenth, fourteenth, and fifteenth amendments. When the Court came to the decision that those amendments were part of the Constitution and that they had been in effect all the time, then it was necessary to enforce that decision all over the country. And an effort was made to do that, although I think the approach was wrong.

Such things have got to be put into effect by leadership, and the leadership has to make it perfectly apparent that what he is trying to do is right and convince the majority of the people of the United States that the leadership is on the right track.

## Legislating Equality: Some Reservations

What we want is political equality and economic equality regardless of race, creed, or color. But when it comes to social matters, a man has a right to pick his associates. He doesn't have to go to parties if he doesn't approve of them. He doesn't have to have people at his house that he doesn't want in the place.

I remember one time in 1940 when I was having the most feverish campaign I ever had and some of these smart-alecks—liberals, they call themselves—came to see me and wanted to know when I was going to invite certain people to dinner. I said, "Never. There are five thousand people in my town I don't invite for dinner. I invite the friends that I want to dinner and you can go and take that for what it's worth." I never heard any more about it.

It's political and economic equality we are fighting for all the way around the world, and when people get that idea, we won't have any more trouble. Social equality, that is a different thing. That is a different thing entirely. I am talking about my own house and home. **I'll decide who will come in my front door and nobody else will do it for me.**

## The Sixteenth Amendment: The Fairest Tax

The government had direct taxes on whiskey and tariff duties on imports but it finally came to the point where they had to have enough revenue to run the government, and that's the reason for the income tax.

I think the first income tax was in the Civil War. I know that's the first one of the federal government. It was finally decided to be unconstitutional, and then they passed an amendment to the Constitution which went into effect in 1912, 1913, somewhere along there.

**The income tax is the fairest tax there is because it makes those most able to afford to pay taxes pay them.**

**The danger to democracy comes not from the masses but from the concentration of wealth in the hands of a few—and the income tax is the best remedy for that.**

*David Gallen*

## Two Very Bad Amendments

I don't think the Constitution has had but two very bad amendments, and one of those was the prohibition amendment, and it was finally repealed. And the other one is the twenty-second amendment, which limits the president to two terms, and next to prohibition it's the worst thing that's ever been attached to the Constitution.

I'll tell you why this two-term amendment was passed. It was passed by a vicious Republican Congress, the Eightieth Congress, in revenge on Roosevelt for serving four terms and it was ratified by the states while the people were still thinking about the war which they had just been through, and the Congress wanted to discredit the president who had served and been elected to four terms.

## And Speaking of the Twenty-Second Amendment

You can't have too strong an executive in the White House because his term is limited. You can always put him out if he gets too big for his breeches.

I don't think it's necessary to put a check on the president. **When you elect a president, you ought to elect a man who knows where he's going and knows how to get there. And if you don't do that, you get what's coming to you.**

## *The Two-Term Presidency*

Washington established the custom of the two-term presidency. He had decided in the first term that he wasn't going to run again, because he'd been severely attacked by the press of his time, but Jefferson and Madison and Hamilton persuaded him to go ahead and run for a second term. After he'd been through his second term, he made up his mind that he just wouldn't take it any more, and he quit. And that established a precedent.

The next president, John Adams, could not have been elected for the second term. But Jefferson was elected for two terms, Madison was elected for two terms. Monroe was elected for two terms. And then John Quincy Adams came along and could not be elected for two terms. Andrew Jackson was elected for two terms.

A president has to carry out an administration that is for the welfare and benefit of the country as a whole, not only in his home affairs but in its international affairs, and when he doesn't do that, he can't be reelected. So why worry about it?

**Four years is a very short time in government.**

## *Terms of Office in the Senate and House: A Proposal*

When the men met to write the Constitution of the United States in order to meet the idea of the states' fair representation, they set up a senate with two members from each state, who represent

29

the state regardless of population. And they set up a manner of electing a House of Representatives by popular vote in districts which would be absolutely free of state domination, and they still are because no governor of a state can appoint a successor to a congressman. He has to be elected to succeed to the Congress.

I think when the president is elected to a four-year term, the House of Representatives ought to be elected with him for a four-year term, because if they're elected for a four-year term, they could serve for two years without thinking about being reelected. Now, whenever a congressman is elected, he begins to run for reelection two years hence and he doesn't have a chance to give the time that's necessary for him to be a proper legislative servant of the people. It would also give the president a chance to have a lower house of Congress, which controls the purse strings, along with him when he is elected.

And I have come to the conclusion that it would be a good thing to elect half the senators at that time for an eight-year period, and then elect another half of them in another four years for another eight years instead of one-third every two years for a six-year term.

What I was thinking about was getting rid of this general election every two years on a national basis. I don't think it's at all necessary, and especially it is not necessary with regard to the members of the House of Representatives.

********

*If the president is not in a fight with the Congress or the Court, he is not doing a good job.*

## REGARDING THE GOVERNMENT

Congressmen represent viewpoints of their own districts and states; it's the president who is supposed to represent the whole country, and if he doesn't, he can't have any luck with Congress. If he does, he can get anything he wants from Congress. Of course there are certain chairmen of committees in Congress whose objective is to hamper a program that any president wants to put over, but if the president has the right sort of program and keeps telling the country that this is the program we ought to have, those chairmen in the long run can't obstruct what's necessary and right in a legislative way.

### *"A Bundle of Compromises"*

Any government is "a bundle of compromises," and when it ceases to be a bundle of compromises, it's either a dictatorship or it goes to pot just like the fourth French Republic did.

Compromise comes out of discussion of every approach to a matter that's before a legislative body. In compromise you try to accommodate many views without surrendering the main principle of what's trying to be done, and through compromise the ablest men try to determine how what they're trying to do will affect the future. Because nobody

31

can prophesy the future—if he could, he'd be
Isaiah.

**The least government is the best government.**
*We should have just as little as we can get along*
*with.*

### Federal Powers

The central government must be responsible for
international affairs; it must be responsible for the
circulating medium, that is, the coining of money;
it must be responsible for the defense of the country: Those three things are fundamental, and the
men who wrote the Constitution understood that.

And when it comes to foreign policy, when it
comes to the fact that international affairs are of
great interest to the welfare of this country—and
I think our forefathers foresaw that eventuality—
then you have to have a government which can act
for the whole people of the United States.

And when it comes to the point where an emergency arises, then you want somebody in charge
who knows how to do the job and take over and
see that it runs.

### Emergency Powers

In times past the great republics have been over-
turned because they always elected a dictator to
deal with the emergency. In the Roman republic
the time came when the dictator became the em-

peror of the Roman Empire instead of the leader of the Roman republic, and that's happened in the overturn of all the great republics. That is what happened to the French after the revolutions of 1789. Napoleon took charge because they were standing still, and somebody had to take over and make the thing work.

In our case, the emergencies have been met due to the fact that emergency powers are usually voted to the president by the Congress when the time is necessary for that to be done, and the president exercises them as the leader of a republic and not as a dictator in order to save the freedoms under which we live all the time.

## Meeting Emergencies

The federal government has to act in times of emergency, and it always has. If Lincoln hadn't taken the bull by the horns and acted as he did, we wouldn't have any republic. When the war in Europe came along and Wilson had to take charge of things, he handled it in a way that had to be done. Franklin Roosevelt did the same thing in the Second World War. But after those things are over, the emergency powers are usually repealed and things go back to their normal state.

When the emergency comes along, the president has got to decide what's for the best interests for the country as a whole and announce what he's going to do, and the people will go along with him a hundred percent in every case. They did during the Truman administration—in the rehabilitation of our enemies and the economic recovery of the free world known as the Marshall Plan, and in the case of the Greek and Turkish situation, when Greece and Turkey were about to be overrun by Communists and we decided they shouldn't do it. The same thing happened in Korea, which was the most important decision that had to be made because at that time, after the United Nations was adopted, it involved the whole world.

Now we've got a situation in Cuba. We've got a situation in the Far East and Southeast Asia. And we've got to have somebody now to meet that situation.

## Doing the Job

You have to make up your mind on what's right, after you've consulted all the information and gotten all the authorities on the subject that you possibly can. Then you've got to find out what it's going to cost; you've got to call in the people who have to appropriate the money and tell them exactly what it's about and why you're going to do it, and in every instance, in my experience, there was no difficulty about getting that part of the program carried out. But the president himself has got to decide on a policy.

Then he's got to go to the Congress and tell the Congress what he needs and why it has to be carried out. And nine times in ten they'll carry it out. [That's one of the difficulties that Wilson had, because he didn't take the Congress far enough into his confidence before he started on the League of Nations. If he had, he'd have carried it through.]

When the Congress and the president are satisfied that their policy is correct, then the next thing to do is to go to the public and tell them exactly what's taking place and what you expect to do. And you don't have any trouble. But if you commence telling the public what you're going to do before you do it, you'll never get anywhere.

**The country has never suffered seriously from the acts of a great president, but it has suffered by the inactions of a great many presidents.**

# PART III

The Presidency & What It Takes
to Be the Chief Executive
of the Greatest Republic
in the History of the World

*You can never tell whether a man is going to be a figurehead or a leader when you nominate and elect him for president.*

*If he understands that he is the chief executive of the greatest country in the history of the world and if he wants to exercise that prerogative, he can run the government. If he doesn't, he can't.*

## THE PRESIDENT AND THE CONSTITUTION

It's a remarkable thing about how various presidents have handled the powers with which they're charged in the Constitution. Especially if the man happens to have lightning strike him and he becomes president.

*David Gallen*

## Executive Powers

The Constitution is the greatest document a government has ever written because the things implied in the Constitution are of much greater use to the republic than those that are set down on paper as limitations to what can be done. The most important implication is the power of the president.

There are only a few paragraphs in the Constitution on the powers of the president—to act as commander in chief; to make treaties with the advice and consent of the Congress; to fill vacancies in the Senate—and the Congress can overrule anything he does when they, by a two-thirds majority, pass a law whether he likes it or not. But then there are implications throughout the rest of the Constitution on what the president can and must do to meet situations and emergencies as they come up. And we've had presidents who could, and those who couldn't.

I think the best example of those who couldn't is James Buchanan, who was president from 1857 to 1861. He hesitated because he felt his constitutional prerogative didn't allow him to do things, and he didn't interfere when South Carolina seceded from the United States, and it backfired, and that brought on the War Between the States. (He also wrote a message on the veto of the first land grant to colleges that's a classic. He said that the situation was one which did not require further education of people, that educated people were always hard to handle, and that he thought there were too many educated people at that time—this was in 1857 or 1858—and that it was time to stop it.)

Every president who's met emergencies, as Jefferson did when he bought Louisiana, stretched the Constitution till it seemed it would crack. But it didn't crack, because it was intended for that very thing to happen. And when an emergency has come along, you'll always find that the Congress has authorized the president to exercise certain powers which are necessary to meet the emergency. Even if they have to enact that legislation after he's exercised it, that's been done too.

### Taking Charge

It's the business of lawyers to interpret documents of government—bills, constitutions, and whatever else is before the courts. And they have a habit of interpreting every *a, an,* and *the,* every comma and semicolon, with the idea of winning a case, but when it comes to the operation of government, in order to meet a situation, all an executive needs to do is read the law, read the Constitutional background for that law, then make up his mind what he wants to do and tell the lawyers what he wants to do and have them find a legal way to do it—and if they don't, do it anyhow, and then they'll find the legal way.

**A strong president has the willingness to decide what ought to be done, and then to put it over regardless of the consequences.** The people always get tired when a strong president is in office and tells them what they ought to do for their own good, and makes them do it. They don't like it. They like to quit.

41

*David Gallen*

## Executive Prerogatives

The president has as much right to interpret the Constitution as has the Court or the legislative branch of the government because it's a three-point government, each one independent of the other, and the president's interpretation of the Constitution is just as likely to be right as the interpretation of the Supreme Court.

Just as he has the right to analyze whether the law is constitutional or not, the president has a perfect right to analyze legislation as it comes up. And when he decides that it's not proper for him to sign it or if it's against his policy, he vetoes it. The only check that the legislature has on him is to override his veto by two-thirds majority, and that is pretty hard to do. The veto power of the president is one of the greatest powers that he has.

## Respecting the Bridle

I don't think any president considered the Constitution a burden. Some of them were kind of like a spirited horse when you put a bridle on him, but none of them ever tried to sidestep the Constitution and throw it out. They met the emergencies in periods when we were in trouble, just as Lincoln did and just as Franklin Roosevelt did, but I don't think any of them ever felt that he had any idea that the Constitution wasn't the greatest document that the government has ever written.

\*\*\*\*\*\*\*\*

# THE PRESIDENT AND HIS ADVISORS

## Kitchen Cabinets

**An effective president is one who is able to use his brains and the abilities of the people that he can persuade to come and advise him.**

Every president has his advisors outside his cabinet, and you can call them what you please. These people stand out of the limelight that shines on the White House and are much more important to the president than those who are in his cabinet and in front of the limelight all the time. They are the president's friends, and they can give him information about what is taking place in the country without any publicity and without being interfered with.

I think it is absolutely essential that a president have people he can depend on for information that he needs very badly. A president has to have people who are close to certain segments of the population—people in the financial section, in the farm section, in the labor section—who will give him a frank statement on what is going on with those segments of the population.

And you can't have a man like that if he is expecting to get his picture in the paper and have a write-up about what he is going to say to the president. He's got to be a man who is willing to be anonymous and who's willing to work to give the president the information he needs to carry on the government.

Of course, the president has to be careful to analyze the people who are around him and exercise

43

his judgment in regard to them, and when it is necessary for one of them to leave, he has got to tell them to go.

### *Nepotism*

Using a family connection for places of responsibility in the operation of the government of the United States, or a state or a county or anywhere else, has been carried on all the time, not intermittently, ever since the government was organized. In this modern time of free government I think it is much better for a man in charge of the places of responsibility to find people outside his family who are best qualified for those positions, and eventually he will find the people he can trust. **The hardest thing in the world is to find a man you can trust.** But there are such men, and I know they can be found, and it's always better to keep the government of the United States a free government without the idea of organizing a dynasty of one family to run the government. I didn't use the family in an official capacity in any way whatever, and none of the family ever interfered with what I was trying to do as a public official from the time I was a county judge all the way through my career.

The most outstanding examples of nepotism in the United States are the Adams family, and the Harrison family and the Roosevelt family. Of course, Teddy Roosevelt and Franklin Roosevelt were cousins and in opposite parties, but then it was really a dynastic program because the great name of Roosevelt was an asset to anybody who wanted to run for office, and I never have believed in that. I don't think it's right and proper. I don't think there's any place for dynasty in a republican form of government.

********

## THE PRESIDENT AND THE PEOPLE

*The public relations of the president of the United States is the most important asset that he has, if he makes proper use of it.*

### Presidential P.R.

Now, the president is supposed to be the best public relations man in the country. He is supposed to have friendly relations with all the members of the various committees in the Congress, particularly when that Congress belongs to his party, and sometimes those chairmen of the various committees in the House and the Senate are not in favor of his program.

What the president must do is get those people with him, discuss the matter with them, and then if they don't go along with him, he has to have what under Roosevelt were called "fireside chats" and under my administration were public statements and see if he can't convince the people without in any way reflecting badly on anybody who is in any other branch of the government. He has got

45

to convince them that the committeemen are wrong in their approach and that his program is for the welfare and benefit of the people. In the long run he will get it done.

When I was in a very serious situation with regard to the Marshall Plan and the rehabilitation of those countries in Europe, I called in all the members of the committee, the minority and the majority leaders of those committees, and discussed the matter with them, and I never had one bit of trouble. When I told them that we would have to spend seventeen billion four hundred million dollars to put this into effect over a four-year period, they were surprised, but when I explained the situation to them, they went along with it and we got it done.

**My definition of a leader in a free country is a man who can persuade people to do what they don't want to do and like it.**

### *"The Common Touch"*

I don't know how you would describe it, what you name "the common touch." I think that what you're aiming at is a man who understands people and the people's idea of what things should be done and should not be done. And the proper thing to do is to treat the people so that the majority of them have a right representation with the government and are treated on a right basis.

Now, there is no way in the world for a man to cultivate that—he's got to know it to begin with and he has to go through the experiences that the ordinary person has to go through in order to raise a family, own a little property, and be a citizen of the republic. It just has to come naturally.

*A press conference is kind of a show, and one of the best there is in Washington.*

### Facing the Nation

The best medium for a president to communicate with the people that he has had up to date has been a press conference, where he answers all sorts of questions, and some of the papers print those things *in toto*.

And the next best way is for him to get on the train and go from one end of the country to the other and tell the people what he thinks. It's like campaigning.

**The presidential office is a continual campaign.** In order to get his program over, a president must continually inform the people of exactly what he is trying to do and he has to keep on informing them. It's just like the Communists say: If you tell a lie often enough, people will believe it. Well, if you tell the truth often enough, they'll believe it too, and go along with you.

### Meeting the Press

I like the press conference. I have a great time with the press people, and I usually found out more from them than they did from me for the simple reason that I knew exactly what they were after and what they were trying to do, and what their bosses were after, and it helped me very much in pursuing the policies which I was trying to carry out for the benefit and welfare of the country.

The president has to be in close contact with everything that goes on. He has to know what the people are saying and he has to know what the newspapers are saying and he has to know what the radio and television are saying, and then he has to meet that head on, because he's the greatest source of publicity in the government of the United States. And when he speaks, everybody listens.

**The more controversy you have the better it is for the big issues, because then you can explain what the people who are against you stand for and what you stand for.**

\*\*\*\*\*\*\*\*

## THE PRESIDENT AND THE PRESS

*If you have a free press, there is no way in the world for anyone to get by with the subversion of the government.*

### *A Free Press and the Publishers' Press*

The country press in Missouri and Kansas and Iowa is the ideal of the free press. The editors own their papers, they have their own opinions; they have a right to put them out. We had a free press in the time of Horace Greeley and Charles A. Dana and James Gordon Bennett and the first papers that were set up. Those were editor-controlled papers that expressed an opinion which nobody had to agree with unless he wanted to. And that's not the case now.

The metropolitan press is a different proposition entirely. The great publishers control that press and they're in cahoots to see that the people get what they think they ought to see, instead of giving them a complete set of news. There are only one or two papers in the country that give an unedited news program to their customers. The *New York Times* and the *Washington Star* are the best examples of that that I know of. Of course, they got mixed up in politics, too—they're propaganda sheets just like any other paper, and the people don't trust them.

The great metropolitan newspapers think they can fool the people by propaganda, but they don't fool them, as the sixty percent of the voters who do not follow the recommendations of the press proves conclusively.

### The Press: Some Comments

Editors in colonial times were responsible for their papers and sometimes got shot for things they said about people, but we don't do that now.

There are very few newspapers in this country, great ones, on which the editorial policy is carried on by the editor. They hire columnists on both sides of the fence and you never can tell what they stand for, most of them.

**When the newspapers are against a public man, it is an asset in most instances, because in the long run it will be shown that they had a prejudice which could not be cured.**

I never cared anything about what the newspapers said about me as long as they didn't jump on my family, and then they got in trouble.

I don't think Mrs. Lincoln had anything to do with urging her husband on to seek the presidency. I think she had a great deal to do with urging him to keep it after he had it, and I think she was very well satisfied and very happy in the White House in spite of what the *Chicago Tribune* and the *New York Tribune* and the *Herald* in New York had to say about her, and **it gives me a pain in the neck when the women in a public man's life are attacked.**

**No man who is in a place of responsibility can pay any attention to what the editors of the papers have to say about him. If he does, he'll never have a policy.** Usually they abuse him when he's right because they believe he ought to do something else, and if he knows he's right and goes ahead with it, it doesn't make any difference how much they abuse him. A man's got to make up his mind what's best for the whole country and not pay any attention to what some special interests want. Those people who pander to the press

50

usually wind up being just ordinary presidents. We've got several of them like that.

**The objective of the press is to sell papers and advertising, and you should always keep that in mind.**

### A Note on Horace Greeley

One of the shining examples of what happens to an editor when he gets into politics is Horace Greeley. He was nominated by the stalwart Republicans and endorsed by the Democrats and made a campaign for president in 1872, and he was thoroughly and completely whipped, and after that was over he lived about three months and lay down and died. He couldn't take it. I think that would happen to most editors if they'd get into politics.

# PART IV

**Manifest Destiny:
On the Building of One Nation
and the Disgraceful Passing of Many**

*"**Manifest Destiny,** slogan to justify U.S. west-ward and southward expansion movement in the 19th century. Coined by a Democratic editor, John O'Sullivan (1845), it was exploited by Pres. James K. Polk when the United States annexed Texas and won lands from Mexico. Later the theory contrib-uted to the acquisition of Alaska, Hawaii, and terri-tory taken in the Spanish-American War."*
—*The Random House Encyclopedia, 3rd Edition*

***Every good president has been an expansionist.***

## EXPANSIONISM

### Claiming the West

You take Georgia and South Carolina and North Carolina and Massachusetts and all those colonies,

Pennsylvania, they all had claims to lands west of their boundaries, all the way to the Mississippi River and as far as the line went between the French and Spanish possessions north and south. The principal policy during the colonial period was to protect the western boundary of the colonies by establishing claims to the various lands that stretched west across the continent. They didn't know how far they would go, but when they got to the Mississippi River, it was decided that that was the logical boundary.

By the end of the 1790's Spain owned the territory west of the Mississippi River all the way to the Pacific Ocean, but then in 1801 Napoleon did some tough talking to Spain, and Spain ceded Louisiana back to France, who'd owned it in the first place. And except for the purchase of Louisiana there might be foreign governments in this part of the United States right now.

## Purchasing Louisiana

Napoleon had always had in view that he would establish a part of his empire in this part of the Western Hemisphere, but after his great losses in the battles of Aboukir and Acre he decided that he couldn't because his naval forces had no way of controlling the ocean. So after Spain ceded Louisiana to Napoleon, what he was really trying to do was to put a thorn in the side of the British by selling Louisiana to the United States. Jefferson jumped at the opportunity and purchased the entire territory for fifteen million dollars—that's three cents an acre—and the legal maneuvering was done afterwards.

Some of these Constitutional lawyers say that Jefferson stretched the Constitution until it cracked, because there was no provision in the Constitution for the purchase of foreign lands. But the greatest thing that was done for the welfare of the republic was Jefferson's purchase of Louisiana to prevent the establishment of a foreign government at the western border of the United States. That was the objective, and eventually the Congress came in and agreed with him. After the fact everybody could see how good it was for the welfare of the country.

### Building a Nation

In terms of expansion west what Jefferson was interested in was to have more landowners—more people who were on the land they owned—because he figured, and he figured correctly, that when a man has an interest in a piece of land under a government, he's much more likely to stay in a mind for a free government than if he is just a tenant. Jefferson was always thinking of the future of the government which he had helped to set up.

(It's how they pacified the Revolutionary soldier, who took that fake money that they'd put out to pay him with and used it to buy land titles, and it was a good thing, it worked out all right. It worked the same way after the Civil War, and under the Homestead Act a man could settle and get title to one hundred sixty acres after he paid the government a dollar and a quarter an acre for it.)

57

## David Gallen

### Redefining the West

After the Louisiana Purchase in 1803 Jefferson sent out an exploration party under Meriwether Lewis and William Clark from the Mississippi River to the Pacific coast and right up to the southern boundary of what's now Alaska, which was the basis of our claim to the Oregon Territory at the latitude fifty-four forty. That was in 1805.

After that, the difficulty came up with Texas, which wanted to become a part of the United States because most of the settlers in Texas were from Tennessee and the South, and it finally happened in 1846. Then the Mexican War came along, and in 1848, in the settlement of the Mexican War, James K. Polk as president of the United States made an arrangement with the Mexican government to pay them for all that part of the Mexican territory that was north of the Rio Grande River— and later, in 1853, the Gadsden Purchase extended that a short distance south—but all that land was paid for and it embraced California and Nevada and part of Utah and Colorado—all that section that was west of the Louisiana Purchase and south of the southern boundary of Oregon.

And forty years after we had laid our claim on Oregon Territory, which the British also claimed, that was finally settled by Dan Webster and, I think, Lord Ashburton on the forty-ninth parallel, though our right claim was fifty-four forty. I think that they both decided that the land west of Lake Superior wasn't worth anything anyway and so they might as well just divide it up.

58

# THE QUOTABLE TRUMAN

## West Into the Pacific

As early as 1860, a treaty was made with the Hawaiian Islands that they would not allow themselves to be controlled by any country but ourselves and eventually the Hawaiian Islands decided that they wanted to become a part of the United States.

Then along came the Spanish-American War in 1898, which gave us another foothold in the Pacific with the Philippines. And with that our trade relations with the whole of the Pacific became predominant. They still are as far as that's concerned, after our winning of the Second World War and the defeat of the Japanese, and it's one of the most interesting evolvements that has been made in the history of the world: this great nation growing from just a few settlements on the eastern coast of North America to the predominant free nation of the world in, oh, a century and a half, I guess.

## A Note on Napoleon

Napoleon had tried to establish the French in this part of the world—he'd tried it down in Haiti and was hopelessly defeated in his effort. The whole island at that time was called Santo Domingo, and that's where his wife came from, or from Martinique, and if he'd been true to her—Josephine—I don't think he'd ever have been overthrown. The only reason he divorced Josephine was because he wanted an heir. Well, he got the heir and it still didn't work. His second wife was the daughter of the emperor of Austria and she was no good. All she was was no good.

59

*David Gallen*

### As for "Manifest Destiny"

I don't like that phrase. I think we were lucky in having the people in the areas around us who wanted to become part of the United States. I think we were just doing what's right.

*******

**How would I mark our paper in terms of the Indian? Zero minus.**

## EXPLOITATION

**Butchers, I call them; Cortés and Pizarro were nothing in the world but butchers.**

### The Spanish in the Americas

Cortés was an adventurer. He took a few male soldiers and landed in Mexico and destroyed the Aztec empire. He murdered Montezuma and nearly all the great leaders of the Aztec empire, and he made slaves of the rest of them.

Pizarro did the same thing in Peru, where they had a very stable and very equalized government for the welfare and benefit of the people. He killed the Incas by tying them to a post and choking them to death with a garrote, which was one of the most cruel ways in the world to kill people, and he made slaves out of the Inca Indians to work the mines for the gold which the Spaniards took back to Spain.

I have no admiration for either one of them.

### The Borgia Connection

The proclamation granting the Spanish the right of conquest in the New World in the name of the Pope was issued by Alexander VI, one of the popes who in fixing up a poison bowl for somebody else drank it himself by mistake, and that's how he died. He was Italian, he was a Borgia. The two Borgias who were noted for all the people they murdered—Lucrezia and Cesare—were his son and daughter.

### Slavery in the Americas

Until the Spaniards and the British and the French came to this country, there was no slavery in this part of the Western Hemisphere. In fact the Spaniards were the first ones to introduce slavery on the American continent, not only by importing the Negroes from Africa but also by enslaving the Indians who were already here.

There were over five million people in this part of the Western Hemisphere at the time of Columbus, and about two million of those were on the North American continent and the rest of them were in Mexico and South America. There was never any slavery in the North American Indian tribes themselves. Not even when they conquered did they make slaves of their enemies, although

61

under certain circumstances they may have tortured them or killed them.

*********

*The natives of the United States should not have been called Indians; only because Columbus thought he had discovered India were the inhabitants called Indians.*

## On the Iroquois in the Northeast

The tribes of the Northeast, particularly the Iroquois and the Algonquins, were a great people. They were working toward an organization that in the long run, I think, would have made them great statesmen and an asset insofar as the country is concerned, had they not been mistreated.

The male individual in the great Indian tribes, like the Five Nations of the Iroquois in New York, was a man of dignity and poise. He had a right to his say before the governing council, and his rights were always respected. The Indians also were very fond of children and they were very, very good to the youngsters as they grew up. They tried to train them, both male and female, to the duties which they considered their proper place in life, although they made the women do all the work and heavy drudgery that was necessary. But after the women reached a certain age, they were looked up to and treated as proper councilors in the tribal government.

The local governments of the Iroquois nations were substantially independent, but they banded together for defense and protection. They had a general government presided over by what would be parallel to our president of the United States and they had a council. And they had a war cabinet, which was also international with regard to the Five Nations in its scope. They had an organization of the fighting men known as the war leaders, and whenever it was necessary to go to war with any of their neighbors outside the Five Nations, the war leaders had control, although the civil control never got out of the hands of the civil government.

They didn't have any compulsory military service. It was a volunteer organization entirely. The warriors were trained as youngsters and taught that it was necessary for them to defend their organization when the time came, and they considered it the greatest honor in the world to fight for the benefit of the whole tribe, the warriors did, and that's the reason they were so highly respected.

## The Shawnee of Indiana

Even before the Civil War and the Homestead Act of 1862 there were those among the native tribes who felt that their lands were being taken away from them. And they were—without compensation. After the colonies became the United States of America, in the Ohio Valley Tecumseh and his people had to fight to save themselves and their lands from "Tippecanoe and Tyler too" [William Henry]

63

Harrison. If you remember, that's how he was elected president.

## The Seminoles in Florida

In the Southeast the Seminole Indians and the Choctaws and Chickasaws were terribly mistreated with Jackson in control (and that's the only thing I hold against Jackson), but they never did succeed in conquering the Seminoles. They have not yet surrendered. I saw their chief the last time I was in Florida as president, and he presented me with a shirt and told me that they never had surrendered to the Government of the United States, and I couldn't blame them.

## The Cherokee and Chickasaws, and the Oklahoma Oil Fields

The Cherokees and the Chickasaws and the Osages were simply moved off their lands and brought over here to Oklahoma, which nobody thought was any good. It turned out to be one of the richest places in the world and made most of them rich, and then the white man stepped in and tried to cheat them out of everything they had, and he succeeded in most cases.

## The Osage Indians at Sibley's Trading Post in Missouri

West of the Mississippi River you'll find that an

effort was made by the Osages, who had been moved to the West, to maintain their lands. In 1808 they finally made a deal with a trader named Sibley and two or three of the other people who made settlements west of the Mississippi, and I understand that Sibley made a deal with these Osage Indians to take all their land between the mouth of the Osage River and the head of the Kansas River, which was western Missouri and eastern Kansas, in return for the privilege of their trading at Sibley's Trading Post down here in eastern Jackson County.

Now I don't know whether that's true or not, but I think you'll find that the deeds to the land in this part of the country show that Chief White Hair, who was the head of the Osages, made that deal, and I had an assistant secretary of the air force or the navy, I forget which, by the name of Whitehair from Florida, who was a great-great-grandson of old Chief White Hair, and he told me that if White Hair hadn't been so easy with Sibley and the rest of these people, his whole family would have been millionaires, because they had some of the greatest agricultural land in western Missouri and eastern Kansas.

## The Sioux

The Indians got cheated every time they got into a trade with a white man. Look what old Crook did—General Crook, for whom Fort Crook in Nebraska is named, and he had the right name. He went out there and got Sitting Bull and Crazy Horse, who were the leaders of the Sioux who had

defeated Custer at Little Bighorn—he got them
into a conference and quoted the president and
said they would get what they wanted and they
didn't get anything they wanted, and they were
both assassinated by Indian police who were hired
to work for the soldiers.

## The Cheyenne

In eastern Colorado Black Kettle and his tribe
were slaughtered by a colonel who was in charge
of the Colorado National Guard. The colonel was
pretty well thought of in his time, but I never
thought much of a man who would in cold blood
slaughter an old Indian and his whole family when
they were moving apparently to the territory which
had been set aside for them in Oklahoma.

## The Nez Percé

And in the Far West, when the Nez Percé Indians
were being mistreated, Chief Joseph marched his
men, women, and children from Idaho to Montana
in an effort to get into Canada. It was one of the
greatest marches in the history of the world, from
the valley of the Salmon River out in Idaho to Montana east of the Glacier National Park. He's one of
the great leaders of all time. Chief Joseph outmaneuvered not only one of the great generals of the
Civil War, General Howard, but also another Civil
War general who was supposed to meet him. They
were four miles apart and neither one of them
knew where the other one was, and Chief Joseph

knew where both of them were, and he got all his people out.

That great dam out in Montana, the Chief Joseph Dam, was named for that old Indian who outmaneuvered the whole cavalry of the United States for eighteen hundred miles. And they never did catch up with him. Finally, after they had killed most of his people off, he surrendered.

### Geronimo

They were all afraid of Geronimo, all the soldiers were. He was the great Apache chief who was trying to save the Southwest for his Apache people. He was a fierce fighter, and of course they called him a murderer and a cutthroat, and he may have been, but he was trying to protect the land for the benefit of his people. And I don't have anything against him for doing that.

### The Forked Tongue

You can't forget the patriotism of these Indian chiefs who were trying to save their land and their people from exploitation by the whites who made treaties with them and broke them every time they made one.

After the Civil War, when the soldiers were offered homesteads in the West—and of course they went out and took up the homesteads—the Indians began murdering their people and running them out. Often families would be massacred, but the Indians were only protecting their ownership of the property which had been taken away from them. Then the federal government took over things and took care of the Indians. They were put on reservations.

The Indians were the owners and the occupiers of the land, and they were treated as a conquered people. Their land was taken away from them and distributed by the government of the United States to the settlers and homesteaders. The whites took all their hunting grounds, and all the places where they could make a living, from them. That's how their extermination came about.

## A Personal Note

I was looking after the Indian rights all the time. Whenever any bill came up that looked to me like it was for their exploitation, it got vetoed. You will find, I think, at least three of them are vetoed when I was president. I think one of them affected Chief Joseph's settlement in Montana and another one would have taken everything the Indians in Nevada had left—all the lands around Tahoe would have been turned loose for settlement.

## A Horrible Thing to Contemplate

The treatment of the Indian tribes and the Indian chiefs by the white settlers of the American continent, both North and South America, is a horrible thing to contemplate.

We had some great Indian chief leaders on the North American continent. There was Pontiac and

Tecumseh, there was Chief Joseph and Geronimo—all of them fighting for the welfare of their people. And of course they were fighting a losing battle from start to finish, in part because of the superiority of the white man's weapons. The treatment of the Indians by the white settlers of both South America and North America was a disgrace and always will be.

They were all almost completely wiped out. There are very few descendants, pure blood descendants, of any of the great Indian tribes which made up the population of what is now the United States and Canada. The Iroquois Five Nations lasted about as long as any of them, but they were finally moved out of their property. It was taken from them by the white people. Then the Cherokees and the Chickasaws in the southeastern part of the United States were moved out to Oklahoma, to the Indian territories out there. The great Sioux tribe of the northern central plains was finally wiped out, as were the Apaches in Arizona, New Mexico, and Southern California.

Geronimo was taken prisoner and held in Fort Sill, Oklahoma, in a little brick building that is still there. If you want to see it, they will show it to you and brag about the fact that this is where Geronimo stayed.

He was one of the great chiefs, old Geronimo was.

# PART V

**The Presidents:
Commentary on the Men
Who Held the Most Powerful Office
in the Land**

*There were faults in the best of them, there were perfections in the rest of them.*

### The Presidents: An Introductory Note

We have to try to understand the men who became president as they were and for what they tried to do, and we have to give them credit for what they did do and criticize them for what they didn't. And that's often hard to find out because the papers of a great many of the presidents have been destroyed, and that's the best place to find out what a man thinks.

The reason that Thomas Jefferson and John Adams are so well known is because of that wonderful correspondence that took place between the two of them and that expressed exactly what was in the minds of the men, one to the other. But a great many of Lincoln's documents were destroyed

73

by his son, and all of Millard Fillmore's were. I don't think that ought ever to happen. I think presidential papers ought to be maintained and kept for historical purposes.

Those men who have had their aims and actions understood are those who made a record of them afterward. If it weren't for Caesar's *Commentaries,* nobody would have understood Caesar.

### Six or Seven Great Presidents

There are about six or seven men who understood the presidency for what it is: the chief executive of the greatest republic in the history of the world. And there are at least that many who paid no attention to their powers and duties; that is, they didn't shirk the fact that they were presidents, but they didn't exercise the powers that were given to them under the Constitution.

I think the strong presidents—and I'll name them, in my opinion, and that doesn't mean that they're the ones—are first of all George Washington, who set up the government, and then Thomas Jefferson, who gave it to the people.

Then Andrew Jackson: He followed a period they called in Monroe's time "the era of good feeling." And when the era of good feeling got to feeling too good, why, the country went to the dogs, as it always does. Well, old Jackson remedied that. You have got to have opposition if you are going to keep a republic running.

The next president who exercised the powers of the presidency as I think they should be exercised was James K. Polk, who bought the southwest part of the country from Mexico for the same price that Jefferson paid for the Louisiana Purchase.

Then Abraham Lincoln, who made a statement that I think is magnificent when he said that he was willing to save the Union if he had to recognize slavery, that he was willing to save the Union if he had to make the country part free and part slave, but that he was willing also to save the Union even if he had to abolish slavery.

**Washington established the government, Jefferson maintained it, and Lincoln saved it.**

After Lincoln the first president who came along that really understood what his job was and worked at it was Grover Cleveland in his first term. In his second term he didn't do so well.

And the next man who came along and really did a job for the welfare and benefit of the country was Woodrow Wilson. And then I was of course highly impressed with Franklin Roosevelt because he met a situation that was almost as bad as the one which Lincoln met, and he was able to make decisions.

**Presidents have to make decisions if they're going to get anywhere, and those presidents who couldn't make decisions are the ones that caused trouble.**

### Some Do-Nothing Presidents

The president can create conditions which will make him great, or he can take things as they are and do nothing. We have had a great many presidents like that: Franklin Pierce, James Buchanan, and Millard Fillmore, and Calvin Coolidge in our own days is the nearest one of the presidents who has been a do-nothing, sit-still president.

The past eight years, I think, have been almost entirely lost because the president felt that he was a kind of monarch who should be above everything that happened in the world and in the country, and that's been bad not only for the presidency but it has been bad for the country and the world as well.

# 1
# THE FIRST PRESIDENCIES

*They say that Washington never won a battle, but he outmaneuvered the British and won the war, and that's the thing that really counts.*

*As Jefferson and Hamilton both said, he wasn't as brilliant as some men ought to be but he knew how to make men behave for the welfare of the country.*

## George Washington (1789–1797)

George Washington was the presiding officer at the Constitutional Convention in 1787. He was the commanding general of the forces that won the freedom of the colonies. And he set up the government as the first president.

*David Gallen*

## General Washington

Washington was a good horseman and a great big man. He was six feet, two inches tall and weighed two hundred pounds. (Lincoln was taller; I think Lincoln was six feet, four inches. Most of the presidents, though, have not been over medium height.)

Washington had been a lieutenant colonel in the French and Indian War, which was fought to defend Virginia and the other colonies from French aggression from Canada. The French owned Canada at that time, and the colonists, who considered themselves British subjects on a par with the inhabitants of England, were helping the British soldiers prevent them from taking over all of the Atlantic coast area. The colonists were mostly small landowners in Virginia and Pennsylvania, in Maryland, in Massachusetts, and Connecticut, and they were protecting their rights. It was a defensive war, the French and Indian War was, and that's how Washington's military career came about.

Washington was an honorable man. His word was better than most men's bonds, and when he told the people what he thought and why he thought it, they believed him and they went along with him. He persuaded the Second Continental Congress to give him money to raise and train a Revolutionary army, and then he persuaded his troops to stay and fight when their terms were up and they wanted to go home. That was one of the great things that he did, he held the Continental Army together after he got it raised.

Washington was really a tough old general when he was commanding the colonial troops. He knew how to command and how far that command should go and when to give it up. He believed in the control of the army from the top, and that's how he made an army of all the militiamen. You see, each state had a militia which was trained for the purpose of defending the colony to which they belonged, and what Washington did was he knit all those militia organizations together, and all the other volunteers who came in, into the Continental Army, which was trained by the German general, von Steuben. Washington was a real soldier and a disciplinarian. When the war was over, the colonial army was as good as any army in the world.

### President Washington

Washington was chairman of the Constitutional Convention, and the men who wrote the Constitution set up an executive because of their experience with the Continental Congress. The Continental Congress was a debating society, and not much more. It had no executive, and so they couldn't enforce their laws, although they passed some good ones.

Washington then became the chief executive in the new government. And he acted like one. When the decisions were hard to make, he made them, and he carried them through. The Whiskey Rebellion was one of the outstanding things which he handled—the whiskey makers didn't want to pay any tax on the whiskey and he made them pay it—and by which he established the right of the Congress of the United States to levy taxes in any way they saw fit, if they were levied by the repre-

79

sentatives of the people. It was the business of the executive to enforce the laws, and he enforced them.

You'll find that in the papers published at that time that they accused Washington of wanting to be king. He could have been if he had wanted to, and he didn't want to. He wanted the republic to go according to the Constitution which he helped to write.

### The First Cabinet

Washington appointed Thomas Jefferson his secretary of state and Alexander Hamilton the secretary of the treasury, and then he later appointed an attorney general, Edmund Randolph, and a secretary of war, Henry Knox. He only had four members in his cabinet, but they were four truly great men. Every single one of them was a man of reputation and highly regarded by the people in the colonies.

I think the reason that Washington appointed them was for the acts they had carried out under the Continental Congress. Jefferson was the foreign representative of the Continental Congress and was familiar with the European situation. Alexander Hamilton was a financier and a great lawyer in the state of New York, and the same can be said of Edmund Randolph, the attorney general. Henry Knox, of course, was one of Washington's generals. Washington knew that he was capable and able to run the War Department of the country.

They were all Federalists in that they were all

in favor of a democratic republic, but they did not all agree on issues, particularly Jefferson and Hamilton, which was all right. Washington is, I think, the only president in history who had a cabinet that was made up of all shades of opinion, and he listened to all shades of opinion, and then he made decisions himself.

### Hamilton and Jefferson

Hamilton was in favor of strong financial control by the central government because the Constitution provided that the states should not have the right to issue circulating medium of any kind. Instead the Congress should authorize the coining of money which would be sound and good in all the states so that they could transact their business and establish free trade with each other. Hamilton was a great man and he was a great first secretary of the treasury, but he had ideas that were as obsolete as King George III's when it came down to running the government.

Jefferson didn't resign as secretary of state because he was falling out with Washington. Jefferson quit because Washington supported Hamilton, which Washington had a perfect right to do if he wanted to and he thought it was right. He was president of the United States and these men were appointed as advisors, not to run the government. I think he was, of course, favorable to Hamilton, because Washington was the richest man in the colonies when they freed themselves from Britain, so he naturally would lean in that direction.

While Jefferson was an aristocrat, a big landowner in Virginia, just like Washington, he was always on the side of the fellow who had no representation—that is, the little people. There was a common belief at that time that no matter how much we may read the Declaration of Independence and say that all men are born—created— equal, most of the people in the colonies didn't believe it. They thought that there was a class that was above the everyday, ordinary people; but Jefferson didn't. That was the fundamental difference between Jefferson and Hamilton.

## A Note on the Origins of the Two-Party System

The Constitution was written with the idea that there would not be any partisanship in the government, but because Alexander Hamilton was the financial director of Washington's cabinet and Thomas Jefferson was secretary of state, there were two viewpoints as to how the government of the United States should be run: that it should be run in the interest of those who were supposed to know more about government than anybody else and who were in control the finances and welfare of the country as a whole; and that it should be run in the interest of those who were working in the fields and on the farms. That was the difference between Alexander Hamilton and Thomas Jefferson, and in the long run it developed into a two-party system, which has been very successful in the operation of this country.

The original Jefferson party was the Democratic-Republican Party, which was the party that believed in the people and wanted to maintain a republic as against a monarchy. It was called "the party of the people." The Federalists were special privilege people who wanted, if possible, to have a special class to run the government and to overlook the people because it was decided that everyday men didn't have any sense about government. Well, along in the 1830's Andrew Jackson dropped the word Republican and made it the Democratic Party, which is still the party that Jefferson and Jackson organized. Then, in 1856, after the Whigs, and the Know-Nothings, and the rest of them had failed their party, John Freemont had a session up in Michigan, and they took the other part of the designation of Jefferson's party of the people and called it Republican, and it was made up mostly of Know-Nothings and has been all the time.

**Never in the history of any free country has there been a time when one party could run that country forever. Because opposition is good for any party.**

## Washington and Congress

Washington was very interested in Congress and finally made an appearance there in regard to a treaty he wanted to discuss. He was trying to comply with the Constitution, which says that treaties shall be made with the advice and consent of the Senate. He was trying to get the advice of the Senate, and they wouldn't give it to him.

The Congress was a succession to the Continental Congress. They were already organized. They knew what they wanted to do. They knew how they did business. They had committees and everything

83

of that kind, and so when Washington went down to get the advice of the Senate on this treaty, they told him they couldn't do business that way, that they had to have a committee and that they'd place the matter before the committee and that then they'd discuss it, and that they couldn't operate anyhow with the president sitting in the Senate.

The old man got up and left and told them they could go to hell as far as he was concerned. He never went back, and after that treaties were drafted and then sent to the Congress for consideration.

Washington was as tough as a bird could be and he used language that the artilleryman understands when he got wrought.

## Washington and the People

Washington was a full-time president. He made tours over the entire country when it took months to get from one end of it to the other. He had to ride the stagecoach, but he visited every single state in the Union himself and made appearances everywhere he went. He wanted to give the people an idea of what the Constitution meant and how it was being enforced.

What Washington was doing in fact was establishing the government, and that's the hardest thing a man can do, and that's the reason he is one of the greatest presidents.

## *Washington and the Press*

Washington never took his pay as president, I am sure of that. He took expense money whenever he was out anything in the interest of the government, but he didn't take his pay. You will find that is historically correct. What was false were the charges in the press that as president he was overdrawing his pay. There were so many false accusations against him, and that was one of them. He was, in my opinion, more roundly abused by the press than any other president since.

The establishment of the freedom of the press in this country was a precedent, and the editors and publishers of that day went haywire on the subject of the president. They worked it to death. They would have been suppressed anywhere else, but both Washington and Jefferson believed in a free press. Jefferson, I think, made the statement that he might not agree with what they have to say about him or about anybody else, but he would not forgo the right they have to say it.

## *Washington's Farewell Address, His Isolationism*

Washington's Farewell Address has been used by the isolationists as a basis on which to work, but I'm very sure that if Washington were alive today he would not be an isolationist. At that time he was trying to protect thirteen little states from being overrun and attacked, and it was just good common sense on his part. There were three million people scattered from what's now Maine to the southern boundary of Georgia when he left office, and they were not in a position to become a loud voice in world affairs. The two governments controlling the world then were France and England, and they were at each other's throats much of the time. Washington was trying to reach a balance between those two governments so as to protect the government of the United States. He thought the less they meddled in the foreign affairs of Europe the better off they would be. That was true at the time, but we outgrew it.

## Washington's Demise

After his presidency Washington went back to Mount Vernon and ran his plantation and went out in a bad storm and caught pneumonia and died. They bled him. These modern doctors say that if they hadn't bled him, he might have lived. I don't know whether he would have or not, but I do know he accomplished his purpose.

**If Washington's administration had been a failure, there would be no United States.**

********

## Three Capitals and a Palace

New York was the first capital because it was located in such a way that the New Englanders and those legislators from the South could reach it as conveniently as any other place. But then, since the Continental Congress had been meeting in Philadelphia all the time, it was decided that they would move the capital to Philadelphia because most of the legislators, most of whom had been in the Continental Congress, were familiar with the place.

Then Maryland and Virginia decided to give up a section of land ten miles square, part in Virginia and part in Maryland, on which to establish a capital of the United States, and to be known as the federal district, which would contain only the capital and transact the capital's business.

When the plans were drawn up for what came to be known as the White House, it was called the Palace, but that name was never really used as it wasn't built for monarchs. Washington himself did not occupy the White House, but he laid the cornerstone. (When we rehabilitated the White House, we tried to find that cornerstone, and never did succeed. I don't know what happened to it.)

The first time the White House was lived in was at the end of the Adams administration, I think in 1798 or something like that—1801. They moved in before the house was finished, the Adamses did, and the diary of Mrs. Adams is most interesting about the inconveniences of the new house—the President's House was then the proper name of it. They didn't have stairs to go upstairs, and they used the East Room to hang their wet wash in.

\*\*\*\*\*\*\*

*David Gallen*

# John Adams (1797–1801)

## *A High-Hat President*

John Adams had been one of the foreign service officers under the Continental Congress. He had been to all the countries of Europe, and his son, John Quincy Adams, was raised principally out of this country. They had come into contact with people in Russia and in Holland when Holland was at the height of its power, and Great Britain and France, and they had a very different idea about government and how the country should be run from those people who had grown up in the colonies under the British rule.

While he was a strong advocate of freedom from England and did everything he possibly could to help free the country from England, he still had the idea in the back of his head that there ought to be a ruling class in the country. He and Alexander Hamilton were in complete agreement as to how the government of the United States ought to be run. His vice president, Thomas Jefferson, was not.

People got tired of Adams before he had a chance to have another term. The people thought he was an aristocrat and a high-hat, and that's the reason Jefferson was able to win in 1800. Adams was so disappointed that he left the White House at midnight, so he would not have to ride to the inauguration of the succeeding president in the same carriage.

# THE QUOTABLE TRUMAN

## *A Near Disaster: The Election of 1800*

Under the original arrangement in the Constitution of the United States they voted for president and vice president at the same time, and the man who got the largest number of votes was the president and the one with the second largest number was the vice president. It was customary then for the vice president to succeed the president in the next election, as Adams had Washington.

In the 1800 election Adams came in third, while Aaron Burr, who was supposed to be running for vice president—but he was a conniver—had maneuvered things so that he had a tie vote with Adams's vice president, Jefferson. Burr refused to accept the office of vice president to Jefferson's presidency, and that threw the election into the House of Representatives. They voted by states. Each state had one vote, and it took a great many ballots—thirty, I think—before they arrived at the point where they were willing to take Jefferson for president and Burr for vice president.

But they had very nearly elected Aaron Burr president of the United States, which would have been just as bad as electing Nixon today.

# 2

# FROM JEFFERSON TO JACKSON

*"The country is saved, Jefferson still lives."*
**—John Adams**

## Thomas Jefferson (1801–1809)

### Jefferson the Public Man

The day before his inauguration Jefferson rode horseback all the way up from Monticello, and I have an idea that he stayed in Alexandria or one of those towns close to Washington and then just rode on into the capital on horseback. He was expecting to ride with Adams, but as Adams had left town at midnight the night before, he just rode up and tied his horse to the hitchrack and walked into the place where he was inaugurated.

He was a very tall man, I think six-foot two or something like that. They painted him as awkward in public appearance. You know, he never made any public speeches. It was Jefferson who established the precedent of sending his messages down to be read before Congress.

And Jefferson's campaign had been conducted entirely by letter, from one end of the country to the other. He had correspondents in every state—the leading men in that state—and that's how he organized the Democratic–Republic Party. There, too, he established what you might call a precedent. He was the only one, I believe, who conducted a campaign by mail.

### Jefferson the Private Man

Any subject you want to mention you will find an article on it somewhere in Jefferson's papers. He was one of the brainiest men of his time. He was interested in science, history, engineering, agriculture, government. He was interested in architecture—he brought back the plans for the Virginia capitol from a little temple in Ines, in France, and just outside Venice he found the model on which he built the Monticello house. He was interested in art and drawing and everything of the kind, and he was also a fiddler. He was a very good violinist, Jefferson was, and in his house back there at Monticello they have his music stand.

He had all sorts of gadgets in his home at Monticello. He had a wind gauge on his roof which registered down in the front hall of the mansion, and he also had his bed fixed so he could pull it up out of the way by ropes when he wanted clear passage between his dressing room and the room next to it. He built a cart with special springs to make it easier riding for his trips back and forth to Washington.

He spent most of the time that he was not in Washington at his home. He brought a great many plants from Europe and started the agricultural program for the United States. He started a conservation program to save the soil of the great state of Virginia and keep it all from washing into the Atlantic Ocean. He didn't have much luck in carrying it out because the generations that followed him were not interested in it. That's the reason Virginia's soil is not so rich as it was in Jefferson's time.

It was Jefferson who made our monetary system a decimal system. He made the tenth part of a dollar a dime and the hundredth part of the dollar a one-cent piece, and there were half dollars and quarter dollars, too, all of which made it a much easier system than the British sterling. Jefferson also did his level best to get the metric system of weights and measures adopted in this country, but that was never done.

While he was vice president of the United States, Jefferson put together his *Manual of Parliamentary Practice,* the manual under which the transactions of the Senate and the House of Representatives have been carried on to this time, with amendments which fit in with the day and age. Jefferson's *Manual* is the fundamental guide to parliamentary procedure and also the progenitor of *Roberts' Rules of Order.*

He was a brilliantly educated man, a graduate of William and Mary College, and a lawyer, and most everything you want to name in that day, except he was not a doctor of medicine, although he could have been. And he was a moral Christian man, though the Federalists tried to make him out to be an atheist. Jefferson took all the directions for the proper kind of life out of the Gospels and the Acts of the Apostles and some of the Epistles and put them together in what is known as the Jefferson Bible, and it's good reading.

For Jefferson knowledge was the most important thing a man could have and he tried to attain as much of it as he could. He had one of the finest libraries in the whole Western Hemisphere because whenever he went abroad, he added the books to it that he thought were necessary for a man to understand and read, and that library was the foundation of the Library of Congress.

He also carried on a tremendous correspondence. I found one letter of his not long ago in which he said he was a slave to his writing table. There are two full volumes of the letters which passed between him and John Adams—and that was only part of the correspondence he carried on.

Apparently he was a very genial man, a good man to have around in any sort of company. He knew how to make people enjoy themselves. In fact, he was too much that way—his friends ate him out of house and home, and he lost all his property because he couldn't keep up with the expense of running it. His house was a kind of hotel. Of course, he was so liberal that anything he accumulated soon disappeared with the people who were taking care of him—and taking care of themselves—and he had a tremendous number of family connections which he felt responsible for, so when he died, all his property was gone. He didn't leave any estate of any kind at all to speak of. At his death he freed all his slaves.

The last words of John Adams when he died on the Fourth of July were "The country is saved, Jefferson still lives," and Jefferson was dying at the very same time.

## Jefferson's Legacy

Jefferson was first and last and all the time the man who believed in the government of the United States as it had been set up under the Constitution. He tried to enforce that Constitution to the best of his ability and to make it work to meet emergencies, which he did when he purchased Louisiana. He was responsible for the establishment of a government in the hands of the people, which the Constitution says is where the power of government resides—it starts off with that very statement.

Jefferson's understanding of free government, a government of the people, and how it can be made to work for the people, I think, was the most outstanding contribution that Jefferson made to the history of the United States.

\*\*\*\*\*\*\*\*

## James Madison (1809–1817)

### A War Presidency

Madison's term as president was an unfortunate one. He was president when the War of 1812 came on.

The British had control of the seas and they were impressing seamen on American trade ships into their navy because, they claimed, they were always citizens of Britain no matter how free the United States may be. If it hadn't been for the Napoleonic wars, they probably would have taken over us. They were perfectly capable of doing it.

Now, Madison had been the reporter for the Constitutional Convention. He had a brilliant mind, and his history and records of the Constitutional Convention are the basis for our understanding of how the convention worked, but when he became president, he was like every other man of considerable brain power and education: He found it difficult to make decisions.

The War of 1812 was the most disastrous for the United States of America. The Capitol was burned, and the White House was burned, and Madison had to flee, and Mrs. Madison, Dolley Madison, had to be sure that the pictures of Washington and Martha Washington in the East Room at the White House were saved.

Madison was the only president who, as commander in chief ever took to the field. He had to, because his generals didn't know what to do or how to do it and the militia didn't want to fight and was even willing to surrender. Because of the isolation of the government of the United States from the rest of the world, they didn't think they'd ever be invaded or that they ever would have to defend themselves, so when the time came they had no military minds to meet the situation. It wasn't altogether Madison's fault.

Madison was not a coward by any means, but as

a president, he was what we might call in these days "a weak sister." He couldn't make decisions.

### *Pickling Pakenham in Alcohol: A War of 1812 Story*

General Andrew Jackson won the Battle of New Orleans, which was the only real American victory of the War of 1812, but it was an unnecessary battle because the war had officially ended two weeks before. What Jackson did was set up cotton bales as a defense, and when the British landed, his men—they were all good shots—slaughtered the British in wholesale. I think there were a tremendous number of British soldiers killed at that battle, including Pakenham, who was the commanding general. He was a lord or duke or something of the kind, and when they went to ship his body back to Britain, according to a story which I have heard at the White House, they pickled him in a barrel of alcohol and tied the barrel to the mast.

Well, the common soldiers down below found out that there was a barrel of alcohol attached to the mast, so they took a gimlet and bored a hole into it and got the alcohol out and drank it. And Pakenham was not in any condition to be buried when he got back to England. That's the story told to me by Franklin Roosevelt.

### *A Note on Dolley Madison*

Dolley Madison's great period was after she left the White House. All the way through the Jackson administration she was the social head of the day in Washington. She was a great lady, and a great many matters were transacted that had been discussed at the functions she held at her house. She was made an honorary member of the House of Representatives. I think it was an honor she was entitled to.

She was the most glamorous of the first ladies. Now Mrs. Truman never had any idea of being glamorous.

## James Monroe (1817–1825)

I think there was an expression of sympathy on Monroe's part for the establishment of a republic in Africa for free slaves of the United States. I think that's how it came about that they named Liberia's capital city Monrovia, after him, but I think Monroe himself was a slaveowner before he went broke. His father had left him a great estate in Virginia, but he was entirely destitute when he came out of the presidency and he lived with his daughter in New York until he died.

The Monroe Doctrine is the only great thing that James Monroe did.

## John Quincy Adams (1825–1829)

The only son of a president to occupy the White House, John Quincy Adams was a very well-educated and very conscientious man. The Spanish territory of Florida was purchased during his administration as president, if I'm not mistaken, and I don't think there was any other event in his administration that was very outstanding.

He went back to Massachusetts after he could not have a second term in the White House, was elected to the House of Representatives, and stayed there for seventeen years.

*********

*One of the greatest things Jackson ever said was that as president of the United States and one of the heads of the heads of the three branches of the government of the United States he has as much right to interpret the Constitution as anyone else, and that's what he did.*

## Andrew Jackson (1829–1837)

### A Return to Populism

Andrew Jackson was a very popular figure all over the country. He was at the height of his career as a candidate for president—in great part because of his winning of the Battle of New Orleans. But also conditions were such that Pennsylvania and New York as well as the West and Southwest were strongly for Jackson because they felt that he was interested in the welfare of little men—that is, the

99

small farmer and small businessman—and he was. They also thought he was trying his best to get the finances of the government of the United States centered in Washington instead of in the hands of the Biddles in Philadelphia.

Jackson's presidency was a return to the real Jeffersonian democracy. You see, the times had become such that the special privilege people were in complete control of the government under John Quincy Adams and Henry Clay, who were both economic royalists. The objective of Jackson was to see that the people who had little farms and little businesses were properly taken care of, so when the Bank of the United States tried to shut off the right of the ordinary man to borrow money, he destroyed the Bank of the United States, and he was perfectly right in doing it.

And when he got in trouble with his cabinet over the action, he fired them all and got another cabinet.

### The Spoils System

The government needs cleaning out every once in a while, and you come along with a strong president and he cleans them out. When the government was in the hands of the Federalists who had preceded Jackson in office, there had never been much of a turnover in the operation of the government of the United States, and Jackson, being a popularly elected president, had the natural opposition of all these jobholders and he felt that he ought to have somebody to help him run the government who was in favor of what he wanted to do. That's all he was doing when he discharged a few federal employees, mostly those in key positions. Jackson felt they would do his administration harm if he left them there. He wanted to make his administration work. He had been governor of Tennessee, and he knew what it meant to have people favorable to him in positions of trust under him.

## *Parting Shots*

In his first administration Jackson had as his vice president the gentleman from South Carolina, John C. Calhoun, who was diametrically opposed to everything that he stood for. When he was out of office, Jackson was asked one time what things he had left undone that he felt he ought to have done, and he said he should have hanged John C. Calhoun and shot Henry Clay.

## *An Early Lesson*

During the Revolutionary War Jackson was, I think, fifteen years old, and some British officer tried to make him shine his shoes and Jackson absolutely refused to do it, and the officer hit him over the head with a sabre, not with the sharp edge of the sabre, but he cut his head a little bit. But it also cut his pride. He never did get over it. Jackson hated any person who was trying to press down on the rights and privileges of the ordinary citizen. That's what gave him the idea, I think, that made him one day the champion of the people.

********

David Gallen

# Martin Van Buren (1837–1841)

## *"The Cautious Dutchman"*

Martin Van Buren was Andrew Jackson's vice president, and he was elected president because Andrew Jackson wanted him to be elected president. He had a very serious situation to meet in the Panic of 1837 which came as a result of speculation in land after Jackson left the White House. Van Buren handled it the best he could, but there wasn't much he could do, because he didn't understand what the powers of the president are.

The panic was one of the principal reasons why he wasn't reelected, but the thing that really put him out of the running was his inability to make up his mind on the admission of Texas as a state into the Union. All the South voted against him on that account, and that's the reason he was defeated. Van Buren hesitated because he didn't know which side the popular opinion would be on. That's why he was known as "the cautious Dutchman."

In fact, he was too cautious. Van Buren was always listening to what might be the result of what he might do. If he had had any convictions on what ought to have been done, he wouldn't have had any trouble, but he was a fellow who tried to keep his ear to give them what they wanted, and you can't do that when you are in place of responsibility, as he was. You have got to make up your mind on the basis of what you think is right and then go ahead with it.

102

# 3
## 1841–1861:
# THE MEDIOCRE, THE MINOR, THE WORST—AND POLK

## William Henry Harrison and John Tyler (1841–1845)

### *"Tippecanoe and Tyler Too": The First Whig Ticket*

The Whigs were the successors to the Federalists and the predecessors of the Republican Party. They were made up of Know-Nothings and Anti-Masons and people of that sort.

William Henry Harrison and John Tyler were nominated on the Whig ticket, which utilized all these splinter parties in order to get them elected, but they had no program and they had no platform.

They had a campaign slogan. It was "Tippecanoe and Tyler Too," because Tippecanoe was the battle where Harrison was general. They made it appear that William Henry Harrison had been born in a log cabin and that he drank nothing but hard cider, and so it was called a "log cabin and hard cider" platform, but he was a very rich man for that time—he had one of the biggest farms in Indiana.

Tyler was the disgruntled Democrat from Virginia who had resigned from the Senate because he couldn't go along with Andrew Jackson.

### The Death of a President

William Henry Harrison put on his general's uniform and rode down to the White House on a horse and read the longest inaugural address ever—an hour and three quarters—and caught cold and died within a month of pneumonia.

All the cabinet members that William Henry Harrison had wanted to put in resigned when Tyler took over, except Dan Webster who wanted to keep his job as secretary of state, and Tyler put in Democrats instead. He was responsible principally for the recognition of the fact that Texas ought to be admitted to the Union.

### The President and Daniel Webster

Tyler was the first vice president to take over the operation of the presidency, and I will give him credit for one thing: He established a precedent.

When old Dan Webster wanted to make him merely the acting president, Tyler let him know that he knew the Constitution just as well as Webster did. He said that the Constitution provided that he was the president of the United States in the event that the president passed on, and that he would act in that capacity. This was a wonderful thing. He was the first one; I was the sixth.

Webster also informed Tyler that each cabinet member had one vote, as did the president, and that the majority ruled. Well, the president informed him very carefully that if they had five or six or seven votes and the president said no, that was it. (Lincoln did the same thing when they voted on the Emancipation Proclamation. All the cabinet voted against it, and Lincoln said, "The *aye's* have it; there is one vote for it and that is the vote of the president of the United States.")

Daniel Webster was Tyler's secretary of state, and he stayed secretary of state for General Taylor and for Fillmore, all the way up until the early 1850's. I never thought he was particularly qualified, but that's a matter of opinion. The boundary between Maine and Nova Scotia was negotiated by Daniel Webster and so was setting the forty–ninth parallel instead of fifty-four forty as the possible boundary between Canada and the United States. Dan and the fellow who were negotiating the thing took a ruler and drew a line from the corner of Lake Superior across the forty-ninth parallel. Dan said that part of the country wasn't worth anything anyhow—and gave away our claim to fifty-four forty.

**Webster was a windbag. He made a great many orations, and I imagine he did a very good job, but he was still a windbag.**

*David Gallen*

## The Law of Succession

When Tyler succeeded to the presidency, Congress passed the law of succession, which made the cabinet the succeeding men of the president, starting with the secretary of state, when there was no vice president.

That continued to be the case until I became president of the United States. I thought that the successor to the president ought to be an elected official, and the law was changed so that the Speaker of the House then succeeded in case there was no vice president, and the president pro-tem of the Senate succeeded the Speaker of the House, and so on down through the cabinet. When the vice president becomes president, there isn't any vice president, and that's the reason for this law of succession.

## A Close Call

President Tyler came close to dying in office himself—by being blown up on the warship *Princeton*. They were trying out a great big new gun called the Peacemaker, and it exploded. Tyler happened to be down below when the gun went off or he would have been killed along with the rest of them—two or three cabinet members were killed on the *Princeton*; Upshur, Tyler's new secretary of state after Webster, was one of them. It was the biggest naval gun of its time, a mortar really. It was an unfortunate accident.

106

## A *Family Connection*

Old John Tyler was the brother of my great-grand-father's father, and so the family as a whole never thought much of him as a president. He had a mean disposition, and the family has had a mean disposition as a result of being related to him. By that I mean stubborn. When a man is stubborn and believes what he believes and carries it out, that's what we call stubborn. (It's not a bad trait in the presidency.)

After Tyler left the White House, he went back to Virginia, and when Virginia seceded, he went along with his state and then became a member of the Confederate Congress. It was a bad thing to do, I think, but then he had his own beliefs, and he was a contrary old son of a bitch.

\*\*\*\*\*\*\*\*

## James K. Polk (1845–1849)

### *The Man Who Knew What He Wanted*

Polk was not active in provoking war with Mexico. The war against Mexico was organized by the people in Texas, and Polk had to meet the situation or lose Texas, and so he met it and Texas was admitted to the Union with agreement that they could be five states instead of one.

The country was divided on the Mexican War because they were afraid that the accumulation of

107

territory in the Southwest would make the Northeast less powerful and that the territory that was likely to be annexed would increase the number of slave states, and it did, of course, but I don't think Polk had any idea of causing a War Between the States.

When the Mexican War was on, Polk decided that the best thing to do was to take the southern boundary of the United States all the way to the Pacific Ocean, and that's what he did with the idea that the people in the territories would then have the same privileges the people had in other parts of the country—they would have the right to vote and they could decide what they wanted at home and abroad, and they did. California, Arizona, a part of New Mexico, and Utah were all in the part of the country for which James K. Polk paid fifteen million dollars.

Polk was a man who knew what he wanted to do and did it. He was an executive like we dream about, and very seldom see. He said he'd serve only one term and meant it. He made up his mind what he wanted to do and he went ahead and did it, and when he got through with it, he went home, and three months after he got out of the White House he died.

Upon his retirement he said, "I now retire as a servant and regain my position as a sovereign." He was absolutely right. I have been through it and I know.

********

THE QUOTABLE TRUMAN

## The Worst Period

The period from Zachary Taylor until after the end
of the administration of James Buchanan is one of
the worst the country ever went through, and it
brought on the War Between the States.

There was no leadership in the White House,
and the center of power gravitated to the legislature, where there were a great many men in Congress whose voices were heard. There was old Ben
Wade, and there was Stephen A. Douglas, and one
or two others who were very verbose in their appearances on the floor of the Congress. While they
didn't make any contributions to the welfare of the
country, they helped to bring on the Civil War.

### Zachary Taylor (1849–1850)

Zachary Taylor was a field general, one of the great
ones, but when he became president of the United
States, I don't think he knew what to do. He
couldn't fail because he had no program.

### Millard Fillmore (1850–1853)

Millard Fillmore was the vice president who succeeded Taylor upon his death. He had been elected
governor of New York in two ways, on the Anti-
Masonic ticket and on the Know-Nothing ticket,
and he was put on the program with Taylor because they thought he would strengthen the Whig

109

ticket in that part of New York. He had no regular viewpoint because he changed with the wind to three different parties, and as president of the United States he didn't do anything that was worth pointing out.

## Franklin Pierce (1853–1857)

Franklin Pierce was a New Hampshire Democrat and was well thought of all over the country. He had been a brigadier general in the Mexican War. He was very popular in the North and was a compromiser with the South, so he was overwhelmingly elected by both North and South.

As president he didn't do very much, except to sign Stephen A. Douglas's Kansas-Nebraska Bill, which repealed the Compromise of 1850 and the Missouri Compromise. And that had more to do with bringing on the Civil War than any other one thing in that period.

## James Buchanan (1857–1861)

James Buchanan was an old bachelor from Pennsylvania who believed that the principal role of the president was to enforce the laws and not to lead the country, and that's one of the reasons why South Carolina was allowed to secede from the Union without interference.

South Carolina seceded as soon as Lincoln's election was confirmed. Now, South Carolina had threatened to secede before. Old Andrew Jackson happened to be president then, and he told them that if they didn't enforce the laws of the United States, he would come to South Carolina and hang them all—and they knew he would, so they didn't secede. If we had had a strong president in James Buchanan's place, the Civil War probably would have been postponed for a generation, but I don't think it would ever have been stopped.

********

### What Caused the Civil War

One of the principal causes leading to the Civil War was the fear of the South that they would be overwhelmed in the representation in the Congress of the United States—that is the reason Texas was admitted with the provision that Texas could become five states, so there'd be ten southern senators in the Senate—and that the industrial development of the North would cause their downfall. Another was the repeal of the Missouri Compromise and the Compromise of 1850 in the settlement of the territory west of the western boundary of Missouri.

Slavery was an economic issue. You may remember that Jefferson had suggested at the Constitutional Convention that slavery should gradually be abolished after 1809, but New Englanders were in the slave trade business and were selling slaves to the South, which had become the great cotton producer for the mills in England and France and depended upon cheap labor—slave labor—to raise their crop and meet the demand. They disobeyed the legal prohibition against the slave trade and instead increased the number of slaves in the South, which was a sad thing that should never have happened but it did. Had the people considered Jefferson's suggestion that slavery eventually ought to be abolished, I don't think there would have been any War Between the States, because it was an economic war more than anything else.

It was the abolitionists of course who made slavery the issue in the war, and that was what caused most of the trouble. A lot of it started with the passage of the Kansas-Nebraska Bill, which gave the territories the right to decide whether they'd be free or slave.

Stephen A. Douglas introduced the Kansas-Nebraska Bill, and the Supreme Court about that time decided that the Missouri Compromise was, after thirty or more years, unconstitutional. The Missouri Compromise of 1820 had allowed Missouri to enter the Union as a slave state. It stated that the boundary in the slave states would be the southern boundary of Missouri, which was the parallel thirty-six thirty. Maine and Missouri came in together, Maine as a free state and Missouri as a slave state; thus the compromise. And then the Kansas-Nebraska Bill repealed that, you see.

The Kansas-Nebraska Bill, which was approved by Franklin Pierce, brought on the difficulty between the Missouri border and Kansas and Nebraska and the West, and that was really how the whole fight started. Old John Brown down here in Kansas, in the Pottawatomie Massacre, murdered some of the people he said were slaveowners and

112

then went back to Virginia where he tried to create a rebellion and was hanged by Robert E. Lee.

**John Brown was a troublemaker. He was a fanatic, a murderer, and a troublemaker. One of the best things Robert E. Lee ever did was to hang old John Brown.**

Back in the 1840s, if we had had the right sort of leadership, I think the war could have been avoided. But we didn't, and no president would take a strong position on slavery because you couldn't be elected if you did. It was politically expedient even up to Lincoln's time, and in Lincoln's time, not to, because it was entirely economic.

The Civil War had to be fought to meet the situation with which the nation and the government were faced, and nobody could have prevented it. I don't care what all the after-the-fact historians say, there was nothing in the world that could have prevented it. It had to be fought.

# 4

# THE PRESIDENT WHO SAVED THE UNION AND ONE WHO TRIED TO HEAL IT

### Abraham Lincoln (1861–1865)

Lincoln wanted to be senator from Illinois worse than anything he ever wanted in his life. He was defeated by Stephen A. Douglas, and when the opportunity came along to be nominated by the minority party for the presidency, he took it.

I don't think he ever had in his own mind an ambition that he could ever be president of the United States any more than I did. I never thought I would be president. I never wanted to be, to tell you the honest truth.

115

## Debating Douglas

On the platform with Douglas in one of the debates Douglas accused Lincoln of selling whiskey over the counter in his country store down in southern Illinois, and Lincoln said yes, he didn't deny that at all, and then he added that Stephen Douglas was one of his best customers and he was glad that he was, and that ended the whole conversation. On another occasion, when Douglas had had the first say in the debate, Lincoln took off his coat and rolled up his sleeves and said he was going to get into the ring now and stone Stephen.

While Lincoln didn't win the senatorial election on those debates, the reports that we have gave him the best of the arguments in nearly every instance for the simple reason that he understood people and he talked to the people more than he talked to Douglas in his effort to get himself elected.

Lincoln didn't succeed because Douglas had the better political organization, but it taught Lincoln something. When it became time for him to run for president on the Republican ticket, he had the best set-up organization there was at that convention in Chicago, and that's the reason he was nominated.

And I think he was just as much surprised as anybody else in the country was when he was finally elected on a minority vote, although he didn't carry his home state.

## Winning Friends and Influencing People— and the Committee on the Conduct of the War

Lincoln was a good lawyer. He knew how to put

forth his arguments so that the jury understood him, and he knew how to win a case. He also knew how to win an election, and he knew how to win the people after he was elected. And he had one of the balkiest Congresses that any president ever had.

A Committee on the Conduct of the War was a thorn in his side the whole time. It was a joint committee of the House and the Senate, and it caused Lincoln more embarrassment than all the battles that all the Union generals lost. General Lee said in his memoirs that the Committee on the Conduct of the War was worth two divisions to the South. Old Ben Wade and this old fellow by the name of Kootz or something like that, a congressman from Massachusetts, and Zachariah Chandler from Michigan—they interfered with the conduct of the war no end. They should have been tried for treason, all three of them. But they weren't. Lincoln was patient with them and took what they had to say, and he managed to make the operation work in spite of them.

### Stretching the Constitution

Lincoln knew the Constitution of the United States and he knew how much he could stretch it, and he did—to the point where it almost cracked. He suspended *habeas corpus* and did several other things he had to do—he extended the Supreme Court from seven to eleven members, if you remember, and appointed new judges in the District of Columbia—in order to save the Union. And what the Emancipation Proclamation amounted to was the confiscation of private property, though that was corrected by the thirteenth, and later the fourteenth and fifteenth, amendments to the Constitution which were passed after the war.

That's why Lincoln was called a dictator and a tyrant, and that's what Booth shot him for. But I don't think he ever went beyond the scope of the Constitution. I think he met the situation in an emergency, which the Constitution provides for, and it was necessary that he did. And the Constitution was restored in its entirety after it was over.

### Battling Melancholy

Lincoln had fits of melancholy. He was bound to, but he didn't have them in public. Melancholy goes with the job—especially in that position when there were thousands and thousands of men being killed on both sides, and his heart was just as strong for the men who were killed on the Confederate side as for the ones on the Union side.

### Defending General Grant

When Lincoln was told that General Grant was drunk in the Battle of Shiloh and under a wagon, Lincoln turned around to the fellow that told him that tale and said, "Get me a barrel of that whiskey for my eastern generals."

### Helping the Spanish Ambassador

I ran across a story one time that has never been published. The Spanish ambassador was having an affair with one of the ladies in Washington, and he'd see her in Lafayette Park. Well, they had a big iron fence around Lafayette Park and one night the ambassador got locked in, so Lincoln went inside the White House and got a ladder and helped him out.

### Speaking at Gettysburg

At the Gettysburg celebration where Edward Everett, as the great man of the day, made a speech for two hours, Lincoln spoke for about four minutes, and he got about that much space in the national papers. The *Chicago Tribune* made the statement that the President of the United States also spoke and that he made the usual ass of himself. Yet the only words that are remembered of that celebration are Lincoln's Gettysburg Address. I guess that shows what the papers know.

### Favoring Atheism

Lincoln didn't believe that the church had the only door to heaven, and Thomas Jefferson had actually the same opinion, and they were both accused of being atheists. Neither one of them was, if you will read what they had to say on the subject.

**I myself always thought there were plenty of doors to heaven and don't think you have**

119

to go through any single one, although I thought the Baptist was the most likely to get there.

## Being Lincoln

He was just a good ordinary citizen of the United States who had a great brain and who spent his odd times, times when he was not trying cases and things of that kind, studying the history of government in the world. He was one of the people, and he wanted to stay that way. And he was that way until the day he died. That is one of the reasons he was assassinated. Because he didn't have the proper guards around him at that theater.

Lincoln was just himself, and that's the sort of man I admire. There is nothing in the world I dislike more than a stuffed shirt. Stick a pin in the shirt and the wind comes out, and then you will find out that he is a counterfeit. There is nothing in the world I dislike more than a counterfeit.

**I want a man to be what he is, and if he isn't he's a counterfeit.**

## The Measure of Lincoln's Success

Had Lincoln not succeeded in preserving the Union, I think there would have been three or four republics in what is now the continental United States. I have always contended that the northeast section of the country would have become the United States under the Constitution. The Confederate Constitution would have operated in the eleven southern states, and I am just as sure as can be that the French would have been successful in setting up their empire in Mexico if the republic had not survived the War Between the States. The southwestern part of the country would then have been taken over by the empire of Mexico, and there is a probability that Russia might have kept its northwest section of the country and established a Russian territory on this continent, which would have been a terrible thing.

So, the greatest and most essential contribution that Lincoln made was saving the Union and preventing it from being split up into four or five nations. I think that is the most important thing that he did.

That, and also the fact that **Lincoln set an example that a man who has the ability can be president of the United States no matter what his background is.**

\*\*\*\*\*\*\*

## Andrew Johnson (1865–1869)

### *Reconstruction, a Southern Democrat, Thad Stevens, and the Radical Republicans*

Andrew Johnson wasn't a weak president, but he was in an embarrassing position. You see, he was a Union Democrat. His home was in Tennessee. He had been governor of Tennessee and he had been a United States senator from Tennessee, but he was against secession. When the national party met in Baltimore and nominated Lincoln again for the presidency, Lincoln, instead of taking Hannibal Hamlin who had been his vice president the first administration, thought he ought to have a Union Democrat from the South, and he took Andrew Johnson. And old Thad Stevens, who was an Anti-Mason, a Know-Nothing, and finally a Republican when the new Republican Party came along, was bitterly against southern Democrats whether they were loyal or not.

Whereas Lincoln claimed the southern states had never left the Union and should be readmitted to the Union and allowed to elect congressmen and senators, Thad Stevens was of the opinion that the South should be treated as a conquered territory and should not be allowed to get back into the Union except as a territory so that Congress would have control of it. He was very bitter against the South; his iron and steel mill in Gettysburg, Pennsylvania, was destroyed by the Confederate soldiers when Lee was in the neighborhood.

Stevens was one of those northern radicals who wanted to pulverize the South, and as the leader of the House of Representatives he almost succeeded in doing it. Thad Stevens and his crowd wanted the people who had tried to break up the Union to be punished by prison, by hanging, and by things of that sort. In fact, they put Jefferson Davis in prison for a while, the president of the Confederate government. They did everything they possibly could to get a great many of the leaders in the South executed. They even went so far as to want to put Robert E. Lee in jail. But I will say this for Grant, he wouldn't stand for it.

I think that what Andrew Johnson and Lincoln had in mind was the proper education and rehabilitation of the slaves so they could become citizens. Lincoln was hoping that the freed slaves could be made citizens by education and would have the chance to be economically self-supporting by providing them with public land in the West, the free land west of the Mississippi River all the way to the Pacific coast. Nobody knows what he would have done because he died too soon, but that wasn't the idea at all of Thad Stevens and the Radical Republicans. They wanted to be sure that the South was oppressed by the people who had been slaves, and that's what brought about a great deal of the ill feeling.

There isn't any doubt that the Negroes were being manipulated by the Radical Republicans. That every Negro was to get forty or sixty acres and a mule is what the people under Thad Stevens made the Negroes believe. It wasn't true and couldn't happen. And never did happen.

As things went along Stevens tried to eliminate the executive as the executive of the United States. There was only one really honest man in Johnson's cabinet, and that was the secretary of Navy—the old man with the whiskers—Gideon Welles. You take every other one of those cabinet members, not a single one of them was loyal to Johnson, and in the ordinary course of events he could have fired them all and put his own cabinet in there, which he ought to have had the right to do and which had been done by other presidents, but the Congress had passed a bill that prevented the president from firing anybody he had appointed to office. And it took nearly twenty years to repeal that and some of the other vicious laws which had been passed by the Radical Republicans and were unconstitutional.

**Thad Stevens was one of the worst men that ever had anything to do with the government of the United States.**

## A Much Maligned President

Had Andrew Johnson had a favorable cabinet and the support of part of the Congress, I think Johnson would have made a good president. He was the best informed man on the Constitution of the United States that has ever been in the White House. He had plenty of nerve and he knew what he wanted to do and he was willing to make decisions. But he had a hostile Congress, he had a hostile cabinet, and he had the press almost unanimously against him because he came from the South. And he got impeached.

When Johnson went back to Tennessee, he ran three times for the Senate and finally got elected. The last speech he made on the floor of the Senate was a humdinger, then he went home and died that same year.

\*\*\*\*\*\*\*\*

# THE QUOTABLE TRUMAN
## Ulysses S. Grant (1869–1877)

He was named by his parents Hiram and took the name Simpson so his initials could be U.S., for United States. He cut a colorful figure, except he was only five-foot six.

## *The Grant Presidency*

**Grant had the crookedest administration that ever was in the history of the country.**
President Grant will never live down the vicious reconstruction of the South as long as you write history about him. He will never live that down because he was president when the worst part of it was going on. I think he was for the carpet-bagging in the South. He was a general. He had conquered the place and he thought that the conquered ought to pay the bill.

## *Grant & Ward*

Grant had a partner, and in 1881 together they formed an organization named Grant & Ward on the stock exchange in New York, and not knowing how the stock exchange worked—it was wide open; had no regulation whatever—it wasn't long until the stock exchange had everything Grant & Ward had, and a lot more besides.

That is the reason Grant wrote his memoirs. He barely finished them before he died as a result of cancer of the mouth. He sold them for five hundred thousand dollars, and I understand that Mark

Twain was a great help in getting those memoirs published. All that money went to help pay the debts of Grant & Ward.


*Grant didn't care anything about anything except his military career. He was impervious to criticism from any side, but not to flattery. He liked flattery. All the generals do. **All the generals like flattery.***

### Some Thoughts on What Kind of Presidents Generals Make

Most of the generals have the idea that they are going to retire someday to a nice post and sit there and wait for their term to end, and some of them think they can retire to the White House and do the same thing.

We've had difficulty with our military heroes. The only military hero who really made a president was George Washington, and he was not really a professional soldier. Old Zachary Taylor didn't know what it was all about and neither did William Henry Harrison, although he didn't stay there long enough to do any harm. The next military hero that came along was General Grant, who had one of the worst administrations that this country has seen. And the same thing is true of the present occupant of the White House. He doesn't know the history of the country. He's a military man with a military education. And that's what the trouble is.

Now, a military career, no matter on what small basis it stands, is the best asset a man can have if he wants to be elected to office in the United

States of America—anywhere from constable to president. We have had some pretty good men with military character in office, men who were civilians before they went into the military, men like Jackson, Benjamin Harrison, Garfield, McKinley. A president ought to have some knowledge of how the military works, because he is going to be commander in chief if he is president, and it helps.

But professional military men, men who have spent their lives as military men or retired as generals, are totally unsuited for the office, because the president of the United States is a man who should be able to understand what the ordinary common man thinks about. A military man can't do that. The professional soldier is educated in an institution that promotes the idea that an officer in the army is better than the private, and the corporal, and the sergeant, and whenever one of these generals becomes president of the United States, he thinks the whole civilian population is inferior to him when they are in fact equals and maybe better.

I think history has proven that professional military men have trouble running a free government. Because the professional military man is used most of the time to being a dictator.

\*\*\*\*\*\*\*\*

### Rutherford B. Hayes (1877–1881)

After Grant we got Rutherford B. Hayes. Hayes's program was not bad. He removed the Union soldiers from the South, as he promised the southerners he would do if they wouldn't oppose him as president. That started the rehabilitation of the whole South, and you have got to give him credit for that. The northerners and old Thad Stevens called him a traitor, but he wasn't.

# 5

# WAITING FOR WILSON

## James A. Garfield and Chester Arthur (1881–1885)

The Republicans had three candidates in 1880 at Chicago. They nominated James G. Blaine, they nominated Grant, and they nominated Sherman. Garfield nominated Sherman in one of the greatest speeches that has ever been made at a convention, and they had thirty or thirty-four ballots. They couldn't nominate anybody. It was tied up, and Hayes called the chairman of the committee at Chicago and said, "Why don't you nominate the man for president who nominated Sherman and made the best speech?" That was James A. Garfield. They nominated him, and in two more ballots he and Chester Arthur were nominated as president and vice president.

I think Garfield would have made a very good president, but he didn't have time. He was shot in the back at the Baltimore & Ohio station in Washington in July.

Then Chester Arthur became president and took nine van loads of White House furniture downtown and sold it at auction for about sixty-five hundred dollars. Nine van loads. Any three pieces of it would be worth more than what he got for the whole load. I tried to get some of the pieces back when I was president, but they couldn't be obtained. People who had them wouldn't sell them at all.

## Grover Cleveland (1885–1889)

### *The First Term*

Grover Cleveland was a great man. He was sheriff of Erie County, mayor of Buffalo, governor of New York state, and was finally, after a vicious campaign, elected president of the United States.

In 1884 was the first time a Democrat had a chance to be elected since 1876, and the Republicans were very anxious and they brought everything possible they could against Cleveland. They wanted to identify the Democrats with Romanism and rebellion, but the issues backfired on the people that brought it up as so many Democrats and Democratic leaders were Catholics. The opposition has always brought this kind of scurrilous stuff into their campaigns because they are inheritors of the Anti-Masons, the Know-Nothings, the Whigs, and the Federalists, who have always been against the welfare of the common people.

In his first administration Cleveland was responsible for restoring the powers of the president after the high court declared that the bill passed during the Andrew Johnson's administration—the bill taking the powers of the president away from him and declaring he couldn't fire any member of his cabinet—was unconstitutional.

I think that Cleveland in his first term was one of the six or seven great presidents in the United States. He acted as the chief executive ought to act. Very few of them have.

## Benjamin Harrison (1889–1893)

You have three classes of presidents: You have great ones, you have those who are near great, and you have those who don't do anything, and Benjamin Harrison was one of them, one of the third-class presidents.

He was also the grandson of William Henry Harrison.

## Grover Cleveland (1893–1897)

### *The Second Term*

In his first administration Cleveland was a man who was very much interested in the welfare of the

131

ordinary man, but after he was defeated in 1888–he had the majority of the popular vote, but he was defeated in the electoral college—he then went to work for the Prudential Insurance Company and became one of the directors of Princeton University.

When he was reelected in 1892, his viewpoint had substantially changed from what it was while he was president the first time. He called out the troops in Chicago when they had the Haymarket strike—the Haymarket riots you might call them, but it was a strike. Then he became very much convinced that William Jennings Bryan, who truly cared about the welfare of the people, was wrong and backed William McKinley in 1896.

## William McKinley (1897–1901)

### A Full Dinner Pail and a War

William McKinley was elected in 1896 on the Republican ticket on the program of a full dinner pail for working people, which was in the same class as the log cabin and hard cider in William Henry Harrison's time. The objective was to inform the laboring people that unless they voted the Republican ticket with McKinley, they would lose their jobs and wouldn't have anything to eat.

McKinley took office on March 4, 1897. The *Maine* was torpedoed and sunk by Spain in Havana harbor in 1898—February 15, 1898—and the Hearst press and a lot of other demagogue press associations in the country really forced McKinley into the war with Spain. The Spanish-American War put us in the class of a world power because Spain lost Puerto Rico and Cuba and the Philippine Islands. Hawaii was also annexed during McKinley's administration—at their request. We didn't do it because we wanted to take them over.

### *Remembering McKinley's Assassination*

I was in Texas when it happened, when McKinley was assassinated, and I will never forget it. I was down visiting my uncle—my father's older brother, he had two boys at this stage—and my brother and myself, and about half a dozen girls, and some stepchildren, and Ralph Truman and I were down there on a visit and I was in Dallas at the time, in September 1901. I will never forget it. The word came that the president had been assassinated by a crank in Buffalo, New York, and of course that stopped all the wheels from going everywhere and the whole world mourned the loss of the head of the United States government.

## Theodore Roosevelt (1901–1909)

Theodore Roosevelt was always very highly thought of by both Franklin Roosevelt and Mrs. Franklin Roosevelt. She always called him "Uncle Ted," and whenever the opportunity presented itself, she was always telling me something about what Uncle Ted did, and he did a great many things for the welfare and the benefit of the country.

## David Gallen

### *Some of the Things That "Uncle Ted" Did*

When the effort on the part of the government of
the United States to make a treaty with Colombia,
which was the government that controlled the Isth-
mus of Panama, failed, Teddy engineered a revolution in Panama and took over the situation, and
that is how we came to build the canal. It cost
us three hundred million dollars. And in 1904 the
Panama Canal was formally acquired by the
United States.

In the Russo-Japanese War, if the Russians had
won the naval battle in the East China Sea, they
would have taken Korea and the Japanese would
have been defeated. But the Japanese beat them
at their own game, and then Roosevelt intervened.
He brought them over to Portsmouth, New Hampshire, and got them to sign a peace treaty in 1905.
That is how he became the first president to re-
ceive the Nobel Prize for Peace.

In 1907 Roosevelt sent the American fleet
around the world. He did have some problems with
Congress when the fleet ran out of money and got
stuck in either Manila or Yokahama, and Roosevelt
said he was going to send them the money anyhow.
It was a contribution to making America a world
power.

In the panic of 1907 Teddy went to see J. P.
Morgan and finally got him to take charge and try
to stop the panic, which was done.

Teddy also made a great publicity stunt out of
being a trustbuster, but in fact he busted very few
of them.

## *Another Thing: The FDA, and Why It's Great*

In 1906 the first federal Food and Drug Administration was established. And it is still necessary because there are more fake remedies advertised on television and radio right now than ever before. All they do is catch suckers. People listen to a bunch of hooey and then go and purchase something that is made up of nothing but sugar and water as a remedy. They ought to enforce the food and drug regulations even more strenuously than they do now.

The American Medical Association are the ones who ought to protect people against such things, but they don't. **Doctors are opposed to everything that is for the welfare and benefit of the common everyday man.** They won't even operate on him if they find out he hasn't got any insurance and is not able to pay them. They let him go home and die.

## *A Not So Great Thing That Teddy Did*

Theodore Roosevelt favored restricted immigration. Everybody on the West Coast thought the Chinese-Japanese Exclusion Act was a good thing, because they didn't want cheap labor in California, or Oregon, or Washington either. But it was a purely economic thing: **The man that has to have two dollars a day can't compete with the one who can live on two cents a day.**

I have always thought American immigration policy over-restrictive.

135

*David Gallen*

## *The Greatest Thing That Teddy Ever Did*

I have always thought that the greatest thing Theodore Roosevelt ever did was in 1912, when he split the Republican party and thus caused the election of the Democrat, Woodrow Wilson, who was one of the greatest of the great presidents.

## **William Howard Taft (1909–1913)**

William Howard Taft had been Secretary of War and had been governor of the Philippines and was a very fine gentleman.

He was a great big man. He weighed three hundred thirty or forty pounds and was tall in proportion, and was as kindly as he could be, but he was really at heart an old-time, backward-looking conservative—one of the men in the Republican Party who was what is called an ultraconservative—and he fell out with Theodore Roosevelt because of that.

When he was nominated again for president in 1912, he was hopelessly beaten. He ran against Theodore Roosevelt and Woodrow Wilson.

\*\*\*\*\*\*\*\*

## *Remembering the Democratic Convention in Baltimore, 1912*

I was cutting wheat in the field at home, a hundred and sixty acres, and there was a little telegraph station over there in the field about a quarter of a mile away. I'd bring the binder around there and tie the lines around the brake and go over and find out what was going on. And everybody was just overwhelmed by Bryan's speech against Belmont—he was the head of the Tammany Hall organization in New York—and I think it is said they got five or six hundred thousand telegrams, and that ended the situation so far as Champ Clark was concerned.

My father was for Champ Clark, as all Missourians were, but Champ shut himself up and wouldn't talk to Bryan or anybody else on this situation. Bryan wanted to be very sure that the backward-looking financial powers were not in control of the government of the United States, and Champ wouldn't see him and talk to him about it. So Bryan got up on the platform—he was a delegate from Nebraska, and the Nebraska delegation had been instructed to vote for Clark—and said he couldn't support Clark and made his famous speech which called for the nomination of Woodrow Wilson. The convention went with him.

Wilson had made a great governor in New Jersey, and he had fired the political boss in New Jersey—Smith—who was trying to tell him what to do, and he was very popular in the country with a great many of the old-time Democrats, although if Clark had played his cards as he should have, he could have been nominated and would have been the first president from Missouri, but he didn't. So when the time came for a decision between the special interests represented by Belmont and Tammany in New York and Wilson, who was supposed to represent the people, they went for Wilson.

********

*Wilson was smarter than anybody else and he knew it and he let them know it. You can't do that when you're running a government.*

## Woodrow Wilson (1913–1921)

Woodrow Wilson was rather a stiff-necked professor of the presidency and a president of Princeton University, where he had written a history of the United States that is still one of the basic sources of information on the government of the United States. He knew his subject better than anybody and he couldn't help but show it. Of course, that doesn't always work so well with congressmen and senators.

### Wilson's State of the Union Messages

Wilson's messages stated his case clearly, and in legislative matters his program was so much in line with what was needed that he didn't have a great deal of trouble with the leaders of Congress. (It was in the war term that he had trouble.)

Wilson spoke in a language that the people could understand, and he was the first president in a long time to go down to the Congress himself to read his State of the Union message. That made a hit with the Congress.

Wilson knew his messages by heart. He didn't read them. He delivered them. I was talking to a fellow who used to sit behind him when he was making his speeches, and he said that Wilson kept one hand behind him and every time he would go

through a point he would put his thumb on his
first finger, and likewise on the next point, and the
next point, and the next point, and the fellow said
he followed Wilson's speeches through, and he
never missed a point. He could repeat exactly what
he had written without looking at the page. That's
a genius it takes to do that.

## Wilson's Politics, and Some Thoughts on Liberals and Conservatives

I think Wilson was a common-sense liberal. I don't
like these synthetic liberals. He wasn't one of these
synthetic yelling liberals who are always talking
liberalism and who act some other way. He was a
liberal who was for the welfare of all the
people. . . .

As for being liberal or conservative, I don't like
either one of the words. They've been so misused.
**Conservative, I guess, has been defined as a
man who wants to keep special privilege in
control while a liberal is one who wants to
take it away from him. Well, I don't think either one of them have had much effect on the
welfare of the country of the United States.**

The healthy and prosperous part of the population never wants to see change, principally because
they control things that they don't want taken out
of their hands. They are called conservatives because they are trying to protect their own interests.
You have got to have an equal balance between the
people who are looking forward to a future im-
provement of the situation as we have it and those
who are trying to hold us to the status quo and

not go forward at all. One is called a progressive
and one is called a conservative.

**Whatever is best for most of the people will
eventually become the policy of the government of the United States.**

## A Liberal Alignment:
## Wilson and William Jennings Bryan

William Jennings Bryan was on the side of the people who have no representation in Washington, the
people the president is supposed to represent.

Had it not been for Bryan there would have been
no liberal program continued in the United States
under Wilson or anybody else. Bryan was the stim-
ulus for the so-called liberal program which finally
came into effect with Franklin Roosevelt twelve or
fourteen years afterwards.

Wilson was smart enough to take over the things
that were right in what Bryan wanted to do and
put them into effect, and that is what he did with
the Federal Reserve Board, which is one of the
greatest things Wilson ever did. His objective was
to eliminate banker control of government finances
and to put the financial program of the government
of the United States in the hands of the government, where it belonged. The board was made up
of people from all branches of the population of the
United States, except bankers.

Wilson, like Bryan, wanted to take the gold standard away from the control of the New York banks
and put the backing of the currency against com-
modities—corn and wheat and oats and clover and
automobiles; goods of any kind—as well as gold, so

that the corner on the gold market could not in any way affect the currency of the United States. He augmented the gold standard so that the circulation medium would be great enough to meet the transaction of business in the country, whereas the bankers in New York wanted to control that medium so they could raise the interest rates, make money scarce, and choke off credit whenever they felt like it.

Wilson and Bryan were on the same side on the subject of neutrality in the First World War, but when the time came that the sovereignty and the welfare of the United States was affected, Wilson did the right thing. When it was necessary for him to do it, when all the foolishness which the Germans performed forced him to do it, he had to meet the situation and do it. But before that he had gone along with Bryan one hundred percent.

### South of the Border

Madero was the newly elected president of Mexico and he was assassinated, and then Huerta grabbed power by military means, not by election, and Wilson of course didn't approve of that.

Then, when Pancho Villa came across the border into New Mexico and killed a number of Americans, Wilson thought that something ought to be done, and when they tore up the American flag in Veracruz, he ordered that landing down there of naval forces and of Army forces under General John J. Pershing for the return of respect to the American flag. (Pancho Villa was never taken, but the expedition made General Pershing famous and resulted in his becoming commander general in the First World War, under whom I served.)

Wilson's show of force was not an act of aggression. Wilson had no territorial ambitions. He was trying to keep the peace on the border and to prevent a dictator from going outside his prerogative as president of Mexico, and he finally succeeded.

Wilson also sent the armed forces to Nicaragua and Haiti, but that needed to be done at the time and it made no difference what the so-called liberals wanted him to stand for. We were looking after the investments that the economic royalists had in those countries.

### A Note on Wilson's Generals

Teddy Roosevelt was very anxious to command a division in France, and Wilson would not agree to it because he thought it was a political maneuver, and it in all probability was. It was a good thing that didn't happen, for before that war was over Teddy died.

Wilson didn't have any political generals. The generals in command of the divisions and all the rest of the setup in the First World War were chosen on the basis of efficiency and their military education.

### A Great Idea, a Sad Failure

When the peace was about to be brought about, Wilson delivered his great speech on the Fourteen Points. It is one of the documents that will always live in history, because his statements in those Fourteen Points, outside the ones that were at the time necessary for the peace of the world, set out his plan for a League of Nations, and the United Nations shows that he was on the right track.

Wilson had the right idea for the welfare of the world as a whole. But he had an awful time putting it over, and he didn't succeed.

**He was a very, very brilliant man.**

# 6

# A REPUBLICAN SLUMP
# AND A STRONG
# DEMOCRATIC COMEBACK

### Warren G. Harding (1921–1923)

I don't like to make detrimental remarks about a man who has been president of the United States, but Harding never did know what the presidency was about.

He was elected to follow a great president, and when men are elected to follow a great president, the people think maybe they will have some relief from the troubles they have had to go through when a great president was in office.

**What Harding gave us he called "normalcy," but that didn't mean a thing. Or it meant to go back instead of forward.**

145

*David Gallen*

## Calvin Coolidge (1923–1929)

Like Harding, whom he succeeded upon the president's death, Coolidge believed that the less a president did the better it was for the country.

He sat with his feet in his desk drawer and did nothing, just sat there and signed bills when they came up, and vetoed some that were against his principles. Coolidge didn't think that the president ought to in any way interfere with the policies of the legislative branch, and yet the president is the man who makes policy for the whole country.

### *Give That Man a Cigar Band*

There are a lot of good stories about Coolidge. There is one in particular that I have always remembered about a friend of his from Massachusetts staying all night at the White House. This friend got up and had breakfast with Mrs. Coolidge and told her that he was a collector of cigar bands, and she told him to go on over to the office and ask Coolidge for a cigar band—Coolidge always went over early to look through the mail to be sure that he knew everything that was going on. So when this fellow arrived and told the president what he wanted, the president took out his cigar box, took a band off one of his cigars, and handed it to the fellow. He didn't give him the cigar.

### *Better Than Nothing*

Here is another good story about Coolidge. When

146

he was governor of Massachusetts, a friend of his came to see him in Boston, and they sat and talked awhile and Coolidge asked him if he would have a drink. He said he would, so Coolidge got out a couple of glasses and a bottle and poured a drink for both of them, and they had it. Coolidge then put the bottle and glasses away, and they sat there and continued talking. Pretty soon another fellow joined them, and the first fellow who had come in told the governor that he thought his friend would like to have a drink. Well, Coolidge got out a glass and poured a drink for the second fellow, who said, "Doesn't my friend want a drink, too?" To which Coolidge replied, "No, he's had one."

*Mr. Coolidge always called his successor, Mr. Hoover, "the great engineer."*

### Herbert Hoover (1929–1933)

Herbert Hoover inherited problems that developed in the administrations of Harding and Coolidge, and he did the very best he could to try to straighten them out. But under the conditions with which he was faced it was almost impossible. When Hoover found an organization like the Reconstruction Finance Corporation necessary, he didn't hesitate to organize it, but generally his measures to stave off disaster were inadequate for the simple reason that he was of the opinion that the president couldn't take positive action to get things done. His viewpoint was that the president was the executive to enforce the laws and had nothing to do with making them, with which I don't agree, of course. But that made no difference in our friendship.

*******

***Franklin Roosevelt was not a great administrator. He was a great executive, but he was not a good administrator.***

*He wanted to be in a position where he could say yes or no to everything without anyone arguing with him or questioning him, and of course you can't do that in our system of checks and balances.*

***One of his greatest assets was his ability to make people believe he was right.***

## Franklin Roosevelt (1933–1945)

### Meeting Emergencies

I think Roosevelt was a great president. I think he did a great job, and history will say that, I am sure.

When he came to office, we were in the midst of an emergency. People thought they were penniless. ( I don't think we were penniless. I think that people thought they were penniless, but when the facts came to light, they were not penniless and never would be.) People were worried about what was going to happen to the country, and when Roosevelt took over, he met the situation straight on with the necessary legislative programs that put the country on the road to recovery from the terrible depression we had in 1929, '30, '31—with all that series of programs in what they call the first one hundred days. Of course, a great many of those things had been started by Woodrow Wilson in his first administration.

And he reactivated the Woodrow Wilson program for the League of Nations when he and Churchill met in Quebec and started to get the United Nations set up.

And he was the man who persisted in a manner which won the Second World War.

## Making Decisions

**Nobody—remember this—nobody knows all the facts on which a president makes his decisions.**
And if other decisions might have been better, they were Monday-morning decisions after the fact. And I think Franklin Roosevelt did the very best he could under the circumstances, and the only thing I am sorry about is that his health failed and he didn't live until the end of his fourth term.

## Breaking a Precedent

Events forced Roosevelt into a third term. The war was on and he was already committed to Churchill and the free world to try to save it. The people were backing him because we had an emergency which had to be met and they were afraid they wouldn't find a man to meet it.

But I personally was against it, and always had been. I never thought the two-term precedent should have been broken, and I think the precedent should have stood. But I am strongly against the constitutional amendment—the twenty-second amendment—which prohibits the president from succeeding himself for the simple reason that the president is like any other executive and when his plans are limited by constitutional or legislative amendments, he is in a bad way.

The same thing happened with the fourth term, and if the fourth term hadn't come about, I wouldn't have been president. I would have been in the Senate, and would be there yet, where the happiest time of my life was spent.

## Saving Russia

I think both Roosevelt and Churchill were anxious to prevent a Second World War, and their efforts failed. They failed because Hitler was, let's say, a damn fool, and if he had had sense enough to go along with them and had had sense enough to accept the chance he had in the Ukraine when the Russians in the Ukraine wanted to join him, there might not have been any Second World War.

The reason Hitler grew to be so powerful right under the noses of Churchill and Roosevelt was because Stalin made a deal with him. If Stalin hadn't made that deal and had stayed with his friends, there wouldn't have been any Second World War. But Stalin went over and met his guy and made a deal with him, and then as soon as the time became right Hitler knocked down Stalin's ears and went back on the deal, and I don't know how Churchill, all by himself on that little island across the English Channel, could have done anything other than what he did do. And I don't think anybody could have prevented the war by then.

If Hitler had used sense, we never could have whipped the Germans. He had whipped France—France had folded up, and Holland, Belgium, and all of western Europe had folded up—and then he went crazy. If he had stayed out of Russia, he would have had the world by the tail, because he had a deal with Russia. When Hitler double-crossed Russia, that's when Hitler became licked.

When the Germans had gotten within reach of Moscow and Leningrad, the objective then of the Russians was to get on the side of the people who could save them. And we did save them. (Of course, after it was all over, they decided they had saved themselves.) We sent six and a half billion dollars worth of equipment through the Caspian Sea and the Persian Gulf to save the Russians. If we hadn't, the Russians would have been pulverized by Hitler. And if Hitler had succeeded in pulverizing the Russians at the time he had a chance to do it, where would we be?

We had to help Russia to save ourselves. That is the only reason we did it. Without the participation of Russia we could not have won the war. If they had stayed with Hitler and Hitler had been smart, there wouldn't have been any chance to win the war in Western Europe. Russia had seven million men in the field and we had only one million six hundred thousand. Do your own figuring.

## *Trusting Russia*

I don't think Stalin became a menace until after the Potsdam Conference. Before that he had been a friend of the West—at Casablanca and Cairo and Tehran, and finally at Yalta. Roosevelt went to Yalta to get peace in the world—not to accommodate Stalin, although he had to have Stalin's support to win a world peace under the United Nations, and it worked. Roosevelt felt, like a great many people of that period, that he had made an agreement with Russia that would stick and that our strength and ability would hold the Russians in check. After my trip to Potsdam I never thought so.

The only reason for the Potsdam Conference was to implement the agreement that had been made at Yalta. When the Potsdam Conference was over and everything had been agreed to, all of us had confidence that Stalin would keep his engagements. But Stalin had come to the conclusion that he was in a position where he could gain his objective without the help of the West. He thought that he was independent, that he was out of danger and could do as he damn well pleased. That's what the trouble was, and after Potsdam he began to break every engagement that he had made. He broke twenty engagements with Roosevelt and he broke thirty-two with me.

You have to believe somebody and Stalin was speaking for Russia, and he was not a hard man to make an agreement with, but I found afterwards that he didn't intend to keep the agreement. I don't know how you are going to try to determine the future and decide on what will happen when a man doesn't keep his agreements.

When the Japanese surrender came about, I made it a point to be careful to keep the Russians out of Japan on account of the way they had acted in Western Europe.

And when the Russians tried to move into Greece and Turkey and Berlin—that was when I made up my mind that you couldn't trust them. The objective of the Communists was of course to take over Greece and Turkey and Berlin, and the situation had to be met, and we met it as best we could—I was told that airlifts would not work in Berlin, but they did. Had we not effectively met them in Berlin, in Greece, and Turkey, we would have been in a bad fix.

And in the Middle East: They had agreed to withdraw their troops from Azerbaijan in Iran, and they didn't do it. So we ordered a fleet into the Persian Gulf and told them we were sending in divisions, and they moved out.

The same thing happened with Tito at Trieste, when he made up his mind that he was going to take over Trieste after these other things took place. And I sent him word to all right come and we'd have divisions there to meet him. He didn't come. That is the only language they understand.

*David Gallen*

## Harry S. Truman (1945–1953)

### *The Postmaster Who Became President*

In 1912, at the time Woodrow Wilson was elected president of the United States, we had a Republican postmaster, of course, in our little town—about three hundred people—of Grandview. She was the daughter of a man by the name of L. C. Hall, who ran a threshing machine in the neighborhood and who was one of the best friends that my father and I had. So they couldn't think of anything better to do than to make me postmaster of Grandview, and I appointed the girl who had been running it all along under the Republican administration to be the deputy postmaster. She just kept on running it. I guess I was postmaster for three or four years. That was my first experience with the spoils system and bipartisanship, and it worked out very well.

At the same time I was the road overseer in Washington Township, along with my father. He was the overseer, and I was his deputy and did the work. I continued it after my father died in 1915, until I went to the First World War as a lieutenant in the field artillery.

### *The Transition: 1952*

I do not regret not running for reelection in 1952. I thought I had done my duty. I had been in politics for forty years and had been in public office in the nation's capital for eighteen years, and I thought that was enough.

In November, about a week after the election, I called in the president-elect and had him sit with the cabinet, and had each member of the cabinet report on the situation in his department and on what needed to be done. I also invited the president-elect to send his budget directly to the White House because I had to make the last budget, with which he would be associated, with my budget director. I also asked him to send over his prospective secretary of state, prospective secretary of defense, and all the rest of the prospective members of his cabinet so that they could have their programs coordinated with the members of my cabinet. It was the first time in the history of the country that that was ever done.

The only problem was that the president-elect also sent Sherman Adams, his chief of staff, over to the White House. I turned him over to John Steelman, who told him just exactly how things worked. One of the difficulties I had with Adams was that he came in and tried to take immediate charge. He wanted to run *my* staff, so I called him in and told him that I was still the president and would be until January twentieth and that he was only there on sufferance, and if he wanted to find out what went on, all right, but if he didn't, then he could go out and sit down in the middle of Pennsylvania Avenue as far as I was concerned.

It was the most orderly turnover that was ever made in the White House.

*David Gallen*

## Dwight D. Eisenhower (1953–1961)

Eisenhower didn't work at the job. He didn't follow through as president of the United States in carrying out the policy that was for the welfare and benefit of the country. Instead, he tried to discredit the fellow who had preceded him in every way he possibly could. It was a pinheaded personal attitude of a fellow who doesn't know anything about politics, and it didn't work. He had to finally approve what was established by Roosevelt and General Marshall and myself as far as the foreign policy of the United States was concerned, although we lost all our friends in the situation which developed when Dulles became secretary of state. Eisenhower tried to let somebody else do the job which he ought to have been doing himself— which can't be done.

**Eisenhower passed the buck; down.**

# PART VI

## On History,
## How It Is Written
## and How It Is Made

*History is a record of events as they took place. It is a record of the men who caused those events to take place, and when it's not presented in a way that people can understand it, then it's a waste of time to try to read it.*

# WHAT MAKES HISTORY

## *Writing History*

History is continually being rewritten, it's continually being reinterpreted, and they've begun that with me already, but it happens to be that I'm still alive and I can head off some of the interpretations that they want to make.

Like anybody else making a record of historical events I express my point of view on the facts as I assemble them, and if somebody else wants to make further investigation and come to a another conclusion, that's his privilege. The conclusion will

159

be affected by the personality of the historian to
some extent, but he's got to try to be objective, and
he must not leave out any facts because another
historian might take the same assemblage of facts
that he has and come to a different conclusion.

When you're writing history, you must have a
point of view and you may have a prejudice—I
have no objection to that—but you want to be careful if you are preparing a study of history. Be sure
you get all the sides before you make up your mind.
Your sources are any records that have been left
by the man who is responsible for making the
events take place. That's why presidential papers
should be accessible—for investigation and con-
firmation of events that have happened—and
ought never to be destroyed. Presidential papers
are the property of the people and ought to be
turned over to them as soon as a man comes out
of the White House. And you also now have news
and current events tremendously well covered in
this country in newspapers and magazines, in television and radio broadcasts, things of that kind,
that you can refer to if you're trying to settle a
controversy and find out exactly what took place
in somebody's administration. You have to try to
get all the information you possibly can on the subject from every point of view.

## *Men make history, history doesn't make men*

*History is made by men who have the welfare of
the people in their minds, and they have to make
decisions in order to get that done.*

## *Making History*

The facts surrounding the decision to drop the
atomic bomb on Hiroshima are being distorted for
a purpose—for a political purpose. The actual facts
have been stated as to what took place and why it
was necessary that the bomb be dropped. Reason-
able men have come to that same conclusion. Those
men who want to discredit an administration or
somebody who had control of the operations at that
time can distort the facts, but I think we have the
record pretty well cleared up on that.

There was only one group that had a view of
the whole operation. That group consisted of the
president as commander in chief, the secretary of
state, the secretary of war, and the secretary of the
Navy at that time, all of whose judgments as to
what had to be done, or what was anticipated had
to be done, were the judgments on which the decision to end the war was made. And that decision
was to drop the bomb—to drop the bomb and end
the war and save millions of lives, American and
Japanese. And that's what happened.

Now, the war between Japan and the United
States was brought on by the Japanese themselves.
They attained their objective in the beginning by
taking over all the Western Pacific governments
that they could get to, but they paid the bill when
the final windup of the thing came and they were
always sorry. You'll find that there are a great
many Japanese, and I've been in correspondence
with some of them, who always say that had not
the military been in control of the Japanese government at the time of the Pearl Harbor event,
there would never have been a war between the

United States and Japan, because we had always
been friends.

Despite their heavy losses at Okinawa and the
fire bombing of Tokyo, the Japanese refused to surrender. The saturation bombing of Japan took
much fiercer tolls and wrought far and away more
havoc than the atomic bomb. Far and away. The
fire bombing of Tokyo was one of the most terrible
things that ever happened, and they didn't surrender after that, although Tokyo was almost completely destroyed. Only after this other event took
place were they willing to surrender.

Some of the people who were exceedingly
wrought up by the war had wanted to try the emperor and take him out as the head of the government of Japan. If that had been done, the
surrender would never have been completed, because there were a million and a half Japanese
that never would have surrendered if their emperor hadn't told them to.

Those who would discredit the administration
put the actions and thoughts of those who had to
make the decision in an entirely different light
from what the facts really were. One shining instance: They said that I suggested to Stalin that
he postpone the Japanese efforts to approach the
Moscow government because we wanted to drop
the bomb. We didn't do anything of the kind, because the bomb hadn't even been brought to its
conclusion at that time and we didn't know
whether it would go off or not. Another thing: No
one had any way of knowing what the Japanese
were going to discuss with the Russians. Their effort was entirely to keep the Russians out of the

war and didn't have anything to do with their making peace.

## Studying History

I have been studying history ever since I was ten years old. I always was interested in events that had taken place in the past, and I read everything I could get my hands on. There were some documents that put the men in the events in a particularly interesting way, and when I'd run across one of them, why, it was better than reading any kind of story you could want, because they were events that actually had happened and they were told by someone who had taken a hand in it. It wasn't the imagination of some novelist or something of that kind.

Had not Julius Caesar and Cicero left their great writings to posterity, I don't think we'd have ever had a chance to find out just how great these people were in their period. They're the best examples I know of men who left a record—Cicero and his orations, Caesar and his *Commentaries*—and they give us a very different viewpoint than we would have had had we depended entirely on the historians of the day, because you are reading the accounts from the men who made that history.

## Failing History

The reason, I think, for the difficulties of Mussolini and Hitler was that both of them were half-baked. Neither of them was a historian, although each one thought he knew all there was to know about Roman history and German history, and that was one of the causes of their failures. They didn't go deep enough into the thing to see what happened to dictators—that when they had their countries under their control, nearly every one of them came to a bad end.

When Mussolini came to power the Italian people were ready for an uprising, and he, in the beginning, made a very good contribution to the recovery of Italy, but the power went to his head, as it does in a great many instances, and he finally wound up hanging by his heels with his head cut off.

There's only one great dictator whose succession continued for several generations—it lasted about four generations—and that was Genghis Khan. Several great emperors followed him—his grandson, for instance, the great Kublai Khan. They were cruel and ruthless in their military operations, but they were men who helped to build up their country. They had the welfare of their country at heart and their conquests benefited the Chinese people, which in that day was pretty unusual.

### *Learning From History*

*While Conducting a War*

The leadership in a republic like ours must be familiar with what has gone before. No matter what they say that history repeats itself, it doesn't. Conditions come about that are analogous to certain conditions that have taken place before, and if the historical situation is understood by the people who have to do the job, it is much easier to meet a situation that is likely to come along.

In my own experience back in the Senate, on the Committee to Investigate the National Defense Program during the Second World War, I happened to know the history of Lincoln's Committee on the Conduct of the War and I was bound and determined not to allow this committee in any way to interfere with the military program of the commander in chief. The objective of my committee was to see that the federal government was obtaining, for the funds expended, value received, and it's estimated that a great deal of money was saved by the investigation of that committee.

Now, after the First World War and after the other wars immense numbers of investigating committees went into things that happened in the conduct of the war behind the lines which, had they been investigated at the time, could have been corrected at that time. I think there were one hundred sixteen investigating committees after the First World War, and all that investigation was a waste of time because the thing had happened and had passed and there was nothing they could do.

There were no investigations of any consequence after the Second World War because that committee of which I was the head prevented it and prevented scandals and miscarriages of action, too. Unless the supply service behind the lines, the construction of camps, the manufacture of tanks and guns, and things of that kind are properly carried on, the commander in chief won't have the tools with which to win a war. The committee helped to win the war, and it made as great a contribution—

I am kind of egotistical when I say this—as the man who commanded a division on the front.


*In Establishing Peace*

Woodrow Wilson is the most outstanding example of a president who took a lesson from history and improved upon it. The greatest of the great kings of France, King Henry IV, was the one who had the idea of a congress of Europe which would keep the peace. He was on his way to put that into effect when he was assassinated, and then it all went to pot. It was never thought of any more until Woodrow Wilson came along with his idea that the governments of the world should have an association in which they could discuss their difficulties and not have to shoot each other to come to a good conclusion.

Wilson was defeated by the isolationists in the Senate of the United States of America. Another effort was made by Franklin Roosevelt when he set up the United Nations, and it has functioned very well up to date, but it's very young and it takes a long time for international programs like this to be implemented.

I have always thought the very fact that we— the greatest free government, then and now, in the history of the world—were not in the League of Nations is one of the reasons the League did not survive and one of the reasons that Hitler and Mussolini were able to rise to power, and that brought on the Second World War.

# THE QUOTABLE TRUMAN

*When Framing a Constitution*

The men who framed the Constitution also took their lessons from history. Young men they were, who made up the Constitutional Convention—there were only two old men in it, or comparatively old, and they were Benjamin Franklin and George Washington; the others were all young men—and they were better educated in the history of government than any other association of men that has ever been put together. They were trying to take advantage of the mistakes of previous governments in the history of the world from ancient times to their own.

## *Imagining History*

The ancient Romans put the whole Mediterranean bowl into one great empire, and as long as the Romans themselves were interested in the maintenance of a government that could make the whole situation operate, they had no trouble. When they got lazy and fat and thought that they ought to hire the people to fight for them instead of fighting for themselves, down it went.

The world is now in similar circumstances. With the United Nations the whole world now is in the position to transact the business of the world just as we transact the business in the state of Missouri with one hundred fourteen counties. Every one of those counties thinks it is an independent state; but it isn't; it is under the government of the state of Missouri. Likewise, all fifty of the states think they're absolutely independent in themselves and can do anything, but they can't. It takes the federal government with the power to act for the benefit of the whole people to make them a nation. And the United Nations I hope will do the same thing for the whole world.

**Healthy competition without shooting each other: That's what we want.**


\*\*\*\*\*\*\*\*


## WHERE ARE WE GOING?


### *Reading the Present*

The old days—those times that brought about the opening of this land and the settling of this land by people who wanted a hundred and sixty acres to live on and make a living—have gone by the board now that we have machinery in the operation of the agricultural industry as well as in every other line. The machine age is now turning farms almost into corporations, and in the long run I don't know how that's going to wind up, because there's no longer a place for the small landowner, apparently, which is what I've been fighting for ever since I've been in politics.

More and more the people have concentrated in the cities, where they are employed by great manufacturing corporations. Sometimes a fellow just stands all day in one spot and screws one nut to a bolt in a car, and that's his business. And what else has he got to look forward to? He may have a little house out in the country and he may have a garden. If he does, he's much better satisfied than the fellow who doesn't.

We need some sort of arrangement where the fellow who works in these industrial plants has a personal interest in what the result will be. I think eventually that will come about because the great corporations have distributed their stock holdings into the hands of these people so they're all becoming interested in what's going to be turned out, and I think that's in the long run the goal we've got to meet.

But the concentration of population in the big city is going to be one of the greatest problems we've got to face in the future. I don't know what we're going to do with them. The great population centers have gone down. They may be surrounded by a fringe of small houses that in the long run won't even last as long as their mortgage calls for and in about thirty years they'll all be slums, and what we're going to do then I don't know.

### Facing the Future

We're up against a situation now where all the territory on the continental United States, and some of it on the outside, has been made into states, and I don't know where the expanding population is going to go. That's one of the troubles we've got to face. The whole area of the Hawaiian Islands is not enough to put in your eye when you compare it to the states on the West Coast. It's so very small, it's not even as big as a county in Missouri.

The problem of the population explosion can be

solved when we decide to spend enough money to create fresh water out of the sea water and when we put those tremendous deserts, which have exceedingly fertile soil in most places, to work to raise food. That's all that's necessary. There are also river valleys still left that have not yet been exploited the way they were in ancient times in the Mesopotamia and along the Nile, and eventually we're going to get things worked out there, too, so they won't be desert and can be made again to bloom.

It's a world problem. And it has to be worked out on an international basis through an association of nations like the League of Nations or the United Nations.

********

## WHERE WE'VE BEEN AND HOW WE GOT THERE: A PERSPECTIVE ON OUR NATIONAL HISTORY

*I have always been an optimist.*

### *"Perpetual Progressivism"*

The establishment of the first college of agriculture was opposed by the president of the United States because he said, there were too many educated people in the country at that time—this was along

170

in the late 1850's—and whenever a man became educated, he was hard to control. That was James Buchanan, and that was the attitude of a great many people, and it always has been, but it was not the attitude of the men who wrote the Constitution of the United States. They didn't want to hold men down. They wanted universal education, they wanted public schools, to make this country great. And one of the first things that a new state always did was to set up a state university.

Progressivism is the result of the fact that we have unlimited great educational opportunities in this country.

The progressive spirit developed in the United States because there was freedom of action and freedom of thought as well as a freedom of communication and a freedom of transportation from one end of the continent to the other. There were no boundaries and over three million square miles of land on which to work and live.

The government grows with the population, it is bound to. It is a continuing process. The affairs of the five and a half million people who were here when Jefferson was president cannot be run in the same way that they have to be run for the one hundred and eighty million people which we have now. The government has had to be reorganized all the time.

Continual reorganization of the government is essential. It has been possible to suggest reforms that have cut down the expense in the operation of the government. In fact we had a commission headed by Herbert Hoover and Dean Acheson, who made recommendations for Common Sense Reorganization Programs which would help the efficiency and the operation of the government. We put in seventy-five percent of their recommendations. The Hoover Commission was continued in the next administration—they left Mr. Acheson off of it, for political reasons—but even the people who were supposed to be politically friendly to Mr. Hoover refused to take any recommendations beyond those that had already been made.

The government always governs best that governs least, but there are certain things that the government has to do. It has to maintain peace and quiet in the country, that's one of the first things it has to do. When laws become effective due to their passage by the legislature and their signature by the executive, those laws have to be enforced, and it takes necessary people to enforce them. The same thing is true of the courts. With the growth of the population the courts have to expand. That's the reason we appoint more judges in the states and territories and more federal judges in the federal courts.

**And that's what the government is for—to serve the people but not to control them.** Whenever government ceases to serve the people for the welfare and benefit of all of them, it ceases to be the right sort of government, and that has been the fight we have had continually to meet ever since Jefferson became president of the United States.

*If there isn't any economic freedom there isn't any political freedom. When the control of all the resources of the country is in the hands of one set of people or one set of families, then you have a mon-archy, no matter whether it is called that or not.*

*Any man who does things for the welfare of the most people is always called a radical. He doesn't necessarily have to be one.*

### The Progressive Spirit: A Heritage

I was always interested in the people who had no pull. I've said time and again that all the great organizations—labor, capital, and everything else—are able to support organizations at the seat of the government for their own welfare and benefit. But there are more than a hundred fifty, a hundred sixty million people who have no one to do that for them except the president of the United States, and when he doesn't do it, then they are in a bad fix.

Jackson and Jefferson and Woodrow Wilson and Franklin Roosevelt—they were the men who stood up for the people who didn't have any influence or property. That's the reason I am so strongly for those men. They did everything they possibly could to give the fellow who didn't have any pull a chance to make his way in this great republic of ours. Every single one of the states from the Appalachian Mountains to the Pacific coast was settled by people who were trying to improve their conditions, and Jefferson and Jackson, Woodrow Wilson and Franklin Roosevelt, were all on their side all the time, all the way.

# INDEX

# Index

# Index

# Index

# Index

179

# Index

# Index

Roman Catholic Church, 6, 7
Rome, ancient, 3, 11, 12, 32-33, 167
Roosevelt, Eleanor, 133
Roosevelt, Franklin Delano, 28, 33, 44-45, 75, 133, 140, 148-153, 156, 166, 173
  breaking of two-term precedent by, 149-150
  "fireside chats" of, 45
  as great executive vs. administrator, 148
  and World War II, 150-152
Roosevelt, Theodore, 44-45, 133-136, 142
royal governors, 20
ruling vs. governing, 20
Russia, 134, 150-153, 162-163
Russo-Japanese War, 134

Seminoles, 64
Senate, U.S.:
  *Manual of Parliamentary Practice* and, 93
  president pro-tem of, 106
  terms of office in, 29-30
  *see also* Congress, U.S.
separation of church and state, 12-13
Sermon on the Mount, 8
Shawnee, 63-64
Sherman, William, 129
Sibley's Trading Post, 64-65
Sioux, 65-66, 69
Sitting Bull, 65-66
sixteenth amendment to the Constitution, 27
slavery, 61-62, 75
  and the Civil War, 111-112
  post-Civil War, 123
social equality, 26-27
Socrates, 12
South Carolina, 110-111
Southeast Asia, 34
Spain, 5-6, 60-61, 132-133
  American colonies of, 20, 56
Spanish-American War, 55, 59, 132-133
Spanish conquest, 61

Spanish Inquisition, 3
Stalin, Joseph, 150-153, 162
State of the Union messages, 138
Steelman, John, 155
Stevens, Thaddeus, 122, 123, 124, 128
Supreme Court, U.S., 42, 117
  chief justice of, 21
  *see also* judicial branch

Taft, William Howard, 136
Tammany Hall, 137
taxation without representation, 10
taxes, 10, 27, 79-80
Taylor, Zachary, 109, 126
Tecumseh, 63-64, 69
television, 48
Texas, 55, 58, 102, 104, 107, 111
thirteenth amendment to the Constitution, 25, 26, 118
Tippecanoe, 63-64, 104
Tito, Marshal (Josip Broz), 153
Tokyo, bombing of, 162
tolerance, 8-9
Trieste, 153
Truman, Elizabeth Wallace "Bess," 98
Truman, John Anderson, 154
Truman, Ralph, 133
Truman administration, 33, 154-155
  and the bombing of Hiroshima, 161-163
  and Communist regimes, 152-153
  handling of Japanese surrender by, 153
  Marshall Plan and, 46
  and Native American affairs, 64, 68
  and the press, 47-48, 50
  public statements of, 45
  and Russia, 152-153
Turkey, 34
twenty-second amendment to the Constitution, 28, 29, 150
two-party system, 82-83
Twain, Mark, 125-126

181

## Index